LEAN MEDIA

How to focus creativity, streamline production, and create media that audiences love

Ian Lamont

i30 Media Corporation
Newton, Massachusetts

LEAN MEDIA

ISBN: 978-1-939924-84-1
Copyright © 2017 Ian Lamont

Published by i30 Media Corporation,
P.O. Box 66121, Newton, MA, 02466.
For more information about this title,
email info@i30media.com or visit leanmedia.org.

Publisher's Cataloging-in-Publication Data

Names: Lamont, Ian, author.
Title: Lean media : how to focus creativity, streamline production, and create media that audiences love / Ian Lamont.
Description: Newton, Massachusetts : i30 Media Corporation, [2017] | Includes bibliography and index.
Identifiers: ISBN: 978-1-939924-84-1 (hardcover) | 978-1-939924-99-5 (paperback) | 978-1-939924-8 (kindle) | 978-1-939924-97-1 (epub) | LCCN: 2017910438
Subjects: LCSH: Mass media. | Digital media. | Mass media and business. | Advertising--Design. | Motion pictures. | Publishers and publishing. | Popular music--Writing and publishing. | Video games--Design. | Creative ability. | Performing arts. | BISAC: BUSINESS & ECONOMICS / Industries / Media & Communications. | SOCIAL SCIENCE / Media Studies. | BUSINESS & ECONOMICS / Industries / Entertainment.
Classification: LCC: P90 .L36 2017 | DDC: 302.23--dc23

Image credits: Author photo by Marc Lacatell, *www.mlacphotography.com*. Stock photography licensed from Shutterstock. Screenshots featured in this guide are used for informational purposes, education, and commentary.

Cover and interior design by Monica Thomas for TLC Graphics, *www.TLCGraphics.com*. Composition by Rick Soldin Print & Digital book Production, *book-comp.com*

Printed in the United States of America.

CONTENTS

LEAN
MEDIA

Introduction

Hundreds of millions of people across the world are familiar with *The Simpsons*. The dysfunctional cartoon family—including dim-witted patriarch Homer Simpson, his rock-steady, purple-haired wife Marge, the brainy but insecure daughter Lisa, and hell-raising son Bart—has been a pop-culture standard for more than 25 years. Even if you haven't watched an episode of the show, you have probably heard Homer's trademark "D'oh!" or some other catchphrase that has entered the popular lexicon.

The Huffington Post is one of the most widely-read online news sites in the United States. Founded by a group of talented collaborators including Arianna Huffington, the site is regarded as a major force in the world of digital journalism, with hundreds of staff journalists, a small army of unpaid contributors, and international editions in Japan, France, and Brazil. It was acquired by AOL in 2011 for $300 million, according to reports.

Led Zeppelin was a British hard-rock band. In its prime, it was one of the top-grossing musical acts in the world, rivaling The Rolling Stones, The Eagles, and The Who. Led by guitar virtuoso Jimmy Page and fronted by the charismatic singer Robert Plant, Led Zeppelin packed stadiums and sold millions of albums in Europe and North America. Dozens of Led Zeppelin songs charted on both sides of the Atlantic, including the 1971 hit "Stairway to Heaven."

If you are above a certain age, you may not have heard of Minecraft. Young people, however, know all about the online virtual world, which lets players collaboratively build elaborate castles, buildings, mines, and other structures. Microsoft purchased the game from its Swedish developer for $2.5 billion in 2014, and claims fans have purchased more than 100 million copies of the game.

What do these four disparate media creations have in common? Certainly, all achieved massive success on a global scale. However, when the creators started work on their respective ventures, no one foresaw how big they would become. *The Simpsons* began in 1987 as short animated clips shown during the commercial breaks of a sketch comedy show on the upstart Fox television network. *The Huffington Post* started out as a niche site featuring political commentary by Arianna Huffington's celebrity pals, using off-the-shelf blogging software. Led Zeppelin's self-titled first album, known to fans as Led Zeppelin I, was recorded in a few weeks in the fall of 1968 after the British rock band toured Scandinavia, with production self-funded by guitarist Jimmy Page and the band's manager. Minecraft was a weekend project started by Swedish game developer Markus Persson, known by his online handle "Notch."

These projects may have had humble beginnings, but the ways in which their creators innovated greatly increased their chances of success. They moved fast, used low-cost methods of production, and kept production teams small and focused. Crucially, they showed early versions of their works to test audiences, and paid close attention to what those audiences liked—and didn't like. This feedback could be incorporated into subsequent releases, and could also help drive marketing and business decisions.

This type of approach to media creation is at the core of Lean Media, a new framework for the development of 21st-century media. While traditional methods of creation and promotion have become extremely sophisticated, leveraging the latest in digital production technologies and advanced metrics, they are prone to failure and can be very costly. Today's media can no longer afford such wasteful approaches, especially considering the highly competitive war for audiences' attention and dwindling revenue in several important sectors.

Take the television industry. It costs millions of dollars to develop a new prime-time program. The writers and producers who create the story and develop the characters are eminently talented, and work with some of the best casts and crews. The experienced studio heads and network executives have all kinds of data to help them decide which scripts to greenlight and what time slots might work best. The networks will pull out all the stops to market the shows. Nevertheless, new programs have a staggering failure rate in the United States.

Of the ten new shows launched by ABC in the 2015-2016 season, six were cancelled by May of 2016, including heavily hyped remakes of *The Muppets* and *Uncle Buck. Of Kings and Prophets* and *Wicked City* performed so poorly, ABC pulled them after just a few episodes. NBC and Fox had similarly high cancellation rates.

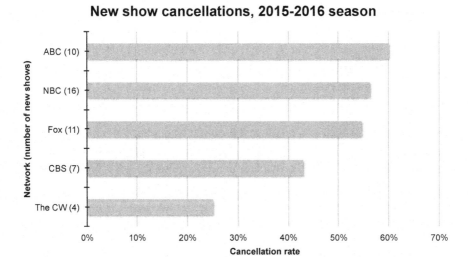

New show cancellations, 2015-2016 season

The system is clearly broken. Nevertheless, year after year the networks and TV studios return to the same outdated modes of program development, counting on a few hit shows to generate enough interest and revenue to stay relevant.

The Lean Media opportunity

The same digital production tools, consumer devices, and distribution networks that are upending the old media world present an opportunity for Lean Media practitioners to focus their efforts and better understand audiences. When applied to new films, music, books, videogames, magazines, online news, and other entertainment and informational media, the framework can bring the following benefits:

- **Concentrated creativity.** With smaller teams and less bureaucratic overhead, a creative team can spend more time pursuing its vision and less time waiting for approvals.

- **Lower costs.** An emphasis on fast iteration and smaller teams leads to faster production, smaller budgets, and more efficient use of resources.

- **Reduction of risk.** The focus on gathering audience feedback early on—and changing course if warranted—means creators are less likely to develop media that flops upon release. Projects that can't be saved are abandoned earlier, saving money and allowing team members to work on other, more promising projects.

- **Media that audiences love.** By the time the media is ready for public release, test audiences have experienced the work during various stages of development, with creators paying close attention and making improvements in response to feedback. It is more likely to be well-received by real audiences when it launches.

While the examples of creative works cited earlier went on to enjoy remarkable success, Lean Media is not just the domain of superstar creators. There are many examples of dynamic individuals working out of a coffee shop or basement recording studio, as well as teams of media professionals working on important creative projects with a limited reach. Lean Media methods can be applied to projects designed for niche or local audiences, or media that has a short shelf life. All kinds of people and organizations can leverage Lean Media techniques to create exciting new media that resonates with audiences and boost bottom lines.

The Lean Media framework has been developed with **entertainment** and **informational media** in mind. It includes formats and programs that were part of the 20th-century mass media landscape, and extends to emerging formats. The list includes:

- Musical works, such as live performances, recorded songs, and music for film, video, and video games.

- Radio, podcasts, and audiobooks.

- Theatrical productions and live comedy.

- Film, video, and animation.

- Fiction, nonfiction, short stories, and illustrated books.

- Magazines, newspapers, and other types of serial media.

- Online and app-based publications, including blogs, online news websites, and niche content providers.

- Video games, from casual time-killers to immersive virtual reality games.

- Advertising and marketing content.

Some readers may regard the scope of Lean Media as being too broad. What could an actor, a news editor, a front-end web developer, and a copywriter possibly have in common when it comes to creating media? My response: While professionals in various media fields have different creative approaches and employ different tools, there are commonalities in the way various media formats are planned, produced, and launched. This allows for a common framework.

Further, with many non-media organizations now engaged in the creation of video, websites, special publications, and immersive media experiences, the framework can be leveraged outside of the traditional media industry. For instance, the clothing company operating a blog about fashion trends can use Lean Media, as can the insurance firm that produces its own monthly magazine for clients. The team of programmers and artists working with an amusement park to design a virtual reality component for a new ride can leverage the framework. Even a local government office that produces a weekly online video series for constituents can use Lean Media to improve its efforts.

It's worth noting that Lean Media is not applicable to two types of non-creative media ventures:

- **Services** for companies engaged in media production. Examples include rights management agencies, metrics providers, printing plants, and equipment rental firms.

- **Platforms** that handle distribution, audience engagement, or specific technical tasks. This includes hardware platforms, such as smartphones using the Android operating system, and companies engaged in exhibition, such as a chain of movie theaters. It also includes social media platforms, which are essentially personal communications networks that can also deliver media experiences.

Certain types of services and platforms may overlap with creative media, such as the artist management firm that produces music recordings or the online streaming platform that commissions its own video content. Talented people working on such initiatives can certainly leverage Lean Media. For everyone else, other business frameworks will be more applicable. For this book, "media ventures" refers to creative media.

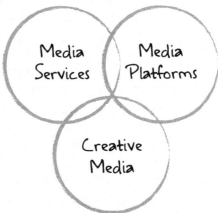

The framework applies to media ventures in the creative realm, but not to service-oriented ventures or media platforms.

A long view of the media industry

My professional media career goes back more than 25 years. I attended the Boston University College of Communication in the late 1980s, and after graduating was fortunate to find employment in various sectors. In the early 1990s, I worked in a professional recording studio in London and was later employed by the independent record label owned by The KLF, one of the top British pop acts of the era. I relocated to Taiwan, where I held positions at a local television network and daily newspaper. Upon returning to the United States in 1999, I found work as a copy editor for IDG, the publisher of *Computerworld, PC World*, and other IT magazines.

By that point, the World Wide Web was well-established, and I knew I wanted my career to shift to digital media. I had already rolled up my sleeves and learned HTML, and in the early 2000s I was hired by Harvard University to help run its alumni website. Later I returned to IDG, working on blogs, podcasts, online video, and a slew of experimental sites including a news aggregator and an online prediction market. In recent years, I cofounded a mobile software company (which failed) and bootstrapped a publishing venture (which is going strong).

When there were opportunities to get involved in a new project or venture, the emphasis was on the practicalities of producing media. There were no theories or frameworks to turn to. The idea was you learned by doing, or perhaps by copying (quoting a radio executive who taught one of my college classes, "The best idea is a stolen idea.") Many times, experienced people on the team showed me the way, by helping me develop new skills or reinforcing professional standards. At other times, I had to learn things on my own, such as when I first got involved coding websites in the 1990s or started publishing books in the 2010s.

As my career progressed, I noticed a growing sense of unease in my industry. New digital technologies were reshaping the media landscape, and myself and many of my peers were anxious about the future. Old media brands that had once enjoyed immense power and profit began to struggle as audience preferences changed and old business models were overturned. The digital media spin-offs created by the incumbents—as well as a slew of new competitors— also struggled to attract audiences and turn a profit.

The 2000s was a tough time to be working in media. In every field, from book publishing to the Web, there was a life-or-death struggle to generate revenue while leveraging technology-driven innovation to connect with audiences. One of my employers, the magazine publisher IDG, furiously tried to adapt to the new online order, but its financial situation never seemed to improve. IDG's corporate leadership implemented belt-tightening tactics, such as eliminating training, restructuring its U.S. business units, and even jettisoning its famous annual holiday party at a big hotel in downtown Boston. It was not enough. Many friends and colleagues were laid off as financial pressures forced IDG and other media companies to downsize and consolidate.

The only players who seemed to thrive were not even media companies. They were Internet services, online platforms, and technology powerhouses such as Google, Amazon, Apple, and Facebook. Who needed a magazine or newspaper subscription when a universe of articles and high-quality information were available for free via Google? Why bother going to a bookstore when Amazon sold the same books for less, and tacked on free shipping to boot? The idea of maintaining a CD collection seemed pointless considering Apple offered hardware and software to import and manage digital music collections and purchase new songs over the Internet. Facebook not only filled a need to stay connected with friends and loved ones, but also provided a channel to share information, bypassing traditional gatekeepers. The platforms were getting ever more powerful and profitable, often at the expense of media companies and individual creators.

The disruption never seemed to end. Just when you thought you understood a new technology and figured out the major players in your sector, yet another upheaval would wash over everything, leaving failed ventures and unemployed media professionals in its wake. Sometimes it was driven by an innovative technology or new platform, while at other times economic forces upset the applecart.

One of the worst weeks of my career took place in early 2009. At the time, I was working as the managing editor of an IDG spinoff based in San Francisco. We were doing all of the right things with the online publication. We had a great team, and we worked with some cool new technologies, including a prediction market that gathered the opinions of hundreds of online users to make data-driven predictions about emerging technologies and business models. We managed to build up a respectable audience, and had some exciting new initiatives planned. But one week in the spring, just as the recession was starting to bite, I received a call from the general manager ordering me to immediately lay off a half-dozen writers on my team. By the end of the week, the GM himself was gone, as was the talented lead designer and hot-shot sales manager. The website limped along with a skeleton crew of just myself and a web developer, and was eventually folded into a sister site.

By the beginning of the 2010s, many people working in media, including myself, saw the writing on the wall. No matter how big or famous our employers' brands were, no matter how good we were at our jobs, no matter how flexible we were when it came to learning new skills, there was a sense that it could all be taken away in an instant. Indeed, overall employment declined, with some industries, such as broadcasting and newspapers, laying off tens of thousands of employees as companies downsized or went out of business.

U.S. employment in broadcasting, newspapers and film

Source: U.S. Bureau of Labor Statistics

What could save us? Established firms and new ventures required new perspectives on the business of media. The old ways of making money—retail sales, print or broadcast advertising, and physical subscriptions—were not cutting it in the age of the Internet and mobile phones.

But there was also an opportunity for new approaches to innovation. As media creators, we were great at leveraging emerging technologies and influences and bringing them into our work. Relentless experimentation yielded great recordings, books, films, television programs, radio shows, serial publications, and in more recent years, a slew of entertaining and illuminating digital creations ranging from electronic music to immersive video games.

However, there was little rhyme or reason to the ways in which we innovated. Many media creators operated in their own bubble, used their own self-designed processes, and played by their own rules. It was questionable whether the approach used by one creator (or a creative team) could be transferred to someone else, even if they were both working with the same type of media. What worked for Beyoncé and her collaborators was not necessarily applicable to Taylor Swift and her team, let alone creative people working in different mediums such as magazines or film.

Moreover, the esoteric communications theories and history lessons I had learned in college provided no guidance for navigating the new business environment or innovating in a smarter way. Neither did the corporate training sessions that I had attended over the years, which concentrated on practical technical skills or touchy-feely soft skills, such as managing change or resolving conflicts.

An introduction to business frameworks

In 2010 I was accepted to a full-time graduate program at MIT's Sloan School of Management. If I were to have a successful career, I regarded a business degree as an opportunity to acquire knowledge that could help me go beyond making media to actually running a business—and navigating the swirling change that was transforming my industry.

It was an eye-opening experience. Unlike my undergraduate education, in which theory was treated in a very abstract sense, separate from the practical aspects of creating media, the business school curriculum focused on the application of theory in real-world settings. MIT's motto is *mens et manus* ("mind and hand"), which emphasizes learning from ideas and practice, whether it be conducting experiments or building something.

Nearly every class involved modeling or prototyping. For instance, in an assignment for our microeconomics class, my team modelled equilibrium prices for high-definition television sets based on classic supply/demand theory. In a computer science course led by World Wide Web creator Tim Berners-Lee, we used an experimental data network known as the Semantic Web to build an educational app for children to learn about animals and their native habitats. In a course about educational games and simulations, I worked with a group of undergraduates to develop a curriculum to teach basic computer science using World of Warcraft, a popular online role-playing game, and new theories about learning in virtual worlds.

A new vocabulary term soon entered my lexicon: frameworks. I learned there are several types:

- **Technology frameworks** are standards-based models that explain how different technology components interact with each other. Understanding technology frameworks makes it possible to design better products, services, and software.

- **Business frameworks** are models for understanding all kinds of management- and business-related topics, such as international competition, personnel management, and strategic partnerships.

Frameworks are not detailed blueprints for designing a product or growing a business. They are also not as intellectually abstract as the communications and social theories I had studied as an undergraduate. Rather, technology frameworks provide a structured approach to solving challenges or implementing new technologies, while business frameworks serve as lenses to better understand various issues related to managing organizations, interacting with partners, and expanding into new markets. Frameworks were tools for creators, managers, and leaders to solve problems and provide strategic guidance.

While the frameworks I was exposed to at MIT were varied, one topic that was not explicitly covered by any of them was media. Yes, it was possible to shoehorn media ventures into a business framework such as Porter's Five Forces or the Innovation Funnel. We could also design an informational website using the technology frameworks underpinning the Semantic Web. Within these frameworks, media was treated like other products and services. However, I felt that some of the unique qualities of media made for a compromised fit.

There was, however, a set of loosely related business frameworks—Lean Manufacturing and Lean Startup—that were different from the others. They came out of industry, as opposed to being hatched by a business school professor or academic research lab. They were more focused on production and customers than other frameworks. While both Lean Manufacturing and Lean Startup were generally incompatible with media production and media audiences, I felt that certain elements could serve the needs of people and organizations engaged in the creation of media. Indeed, exposure to these ideas led to the development of the Lean Media framework.

Understanding Lean Media, from theory to practice

In the chapters that follow, you will not only learn about Lean Media, but also will learn how to apply it to your own projects and ventures. The first part of the book will introduce you to lean thinking in manufacturing and technology startups, and explore the rapid transformation of various sectors in recent decades. The chapters on theory wrap up with the three Lean Media principles as well as the Lean Media flowchart, which illustrate core concepts that underlie the framework.

The second part of the book delves into practical approaches to forming teams, understanding audiences, gathering feedback, and iterative media development. I dig into the scenarios in which media creators may have to pivot or even abandon a work in progress, before covering the Lean Media project planner, which teams can use to further their own projects. Throughout the book, there are many examples of Lean Media in action, ranging from small-scale works to major productions.

Ideally, you will be able to take these ideas back to your own places of employment and apply them to real-life projects. Certain practices may seem strange, such as asking test audiences to look at an unfinished draft or rough cut, or to work with a stripped-down team on a much faster development time-line. But it won't take long to realize these new ways of working can yield real results in terms of cost savings, less bureaucracy, and the creation of media that audiences love.

LEAN
MEDIA

CHAPTER 1

Lean thinking in manufacturing and tech startups

I was introduced to lean business theories while attending MIT. One of my supply chain management instructors, Charles Fine, mentioned Lean Manufacturing (also known as Lean Production) in a discussion of different approaches to producing textiles, electronics, and other factory-made goods.

Lean Manufacturing is an established concept in heavy industry, emerging from the study of successful Japanese companies in the 1970s and 1980s. At the time, there was widespread angst in North America and Europe over unexpected gains by Japanese auto and electronics manufacturers. Business leaders in the West wanted to understand why Japanese industry was doing so well.

It turned out the Japanese companies' success wasn't only because of superior product quality, the cozy relationships among Japanese industrial conglomerates, or favorable exchange rates for Japanese exports. At certain Japanese companies, there was a mindset that emphasized eliminating waste on the factory floor, in corporate offices, and even at suppliers' facilities.

Eliminating waste is the core concept behind Lean Manufacturing. It had arisen in Japan owing to a corporate culture that prized harmony and consensus over wasteful internal conflict and rivalry as well as the country's limited access to natural resources. Imagine working for a Japanese car manufacturer in the 1960s, and having to deal with impediments like this:

- No oil or natural gas meant high prices for electricity and imported fuel.

- Most metals, minerals, and other raw materials had to be imported.

- Wealthy Western countries placed high tariffs on certain classes of imported goods to protect their own domestic industries.

Lean Manufacturing did not address these specific issues. However, it did help some Japanese companies become more efficient, competitive, and innovative. This, in turn, helped them compete in global markets.

The poster child for Lean Manufacturing is the Toyota Production System. The auto manufacturer's website gives the following definition:

A production system which is steeped in the philosophy of "the complete elimination of all waste" imbuing all aspects of production in pursuit of the most efficient methods.

The Toyota Production System extends the idea of eliminating waste into key principles that guide operations. There is *jidoka* ("automation with a human touch") and *genchi genbutsu*, a method of identifying and overcoming obstacles that requires observing problems first-hand, whether on the factory floor or on the road. Toyota also pioneered just-in-time manufacturing (JIT), which emphasizes making only what is needed in the amount required. Toyota's *kanban* process serves as a production control system for managing JIT and making full use of its workforce. In sum, Lean Manufacturing allows Toyota, Nissan, Suzuki, and other producers to operate more efficiently by limiting inventory, increasing collaboration, streamlining assembly line operations, and reducing costs.

Standard criteria for success and failure in media

Lean Manufacturing is certainly interesting. However, while studying it, I did not immediately see how it could be applied to making media. With the possible exceptions of print publishers and DVD manufacturers, few media companies need to consider a supply-chain management framework from Japan. I considered a lesson from heavy industry to be about as relevant to my world as flying a rocket to the moon.

My attitude reflected a certain degree of arrogance and complacency. When it came to success or failure in the media industry, I thought I knew it all, thanks to decades of experience. Not only had I created media and launched new media ventures, but I had also witnessed first-hand the disruption wrought by a host of new technologies. As a battle-scarred veteran, I had seen success and failure up close, and understood how the system worked . . . or so I thought.

For instance, if I had to evaluate the chances of a new album, a just-launched website, or a TV pilot succeeding, I took into account a standard list of factors that I had personally encountered or observed. In my mind, failure could almost always be attributed to:

- Botched execution

- Dysfunctional teams

- A lack of management buy-in

- Poor marketing

- Competitive factors

Conversely, successes usually resulted from having a strong creative team coupled with a solid vision, not to mention good timing. External forces such as new technologies, shifting audience preferences, and economic conditions could also play a role in making or breaking a new media project.

Consider *Wired*, a magazine founded in the mid-1990s. It not only had a strong editorial and design team, but the content also was guided by a fabulous vision to make a once geeky subject area (science and technology) sexy and cool. The articles and interviews were thought-provoking and well-written. The photographs, visualizations, and graphic design was gorgeous. Even the advertisements were eye-catching and different.

Wired launched at an ideal time—the World Wide Web, mobile phones, and powerful 3D games had recently exploded into the mainstream consciousness. Society was ready for a magazine like *Wired*. It quickly became a top-selling title.

The success of *The Simpsons* could also be viewed through the lens of team, vision, and timing. The show not only had a group of visionary creators, eccentric animators, and crack writers, but also entered a broadcasting landscape that had long ago relegated cartoons to a kid-dominated Saturday morning audience. In order to differentiate its programming in a field dominated by established broadcast networks, the newly launched Fox Broadcasting Company was willing to make some big bets on unconventional prime-time programming. Executives gave *The Simpsons* a chance. It became a breakout hit, not just among kids, but among adults, too.

When it came to small-scale projects I had worked on, the same factors applied. In the mid-2000s, I launched a special branded blog on Computerworld.

com called *IT Blogwatch*. The vision: Create an entertaining daily summary of the best technology blog posts so readers would not have to hunt them down on their own. The creative team consisted of myself as editor and a witty British blogger named Richi Jennings who could prepare a new edition every morning before tech workers on the East Coast rolled out of bed. The timing was ideal. Blogs were just starting to take off. People realized the value of expert voices from across the Web opining on various technology topics. *IT Blogwatch* became the centerpiece of *Computerworld* blogs, and racked up more than 40 million page views in its first ten years. The site was an example of vision, team, audience dynamics, and timing coming together to make great media.

Eric Ries and the Lean Startup

I had assumed that "lean" in the business world boiled down to streamlining manufacturing operations. I was wrong. Not long after the supply chain management class ended, my view of lean concepts, not to mention my pre-existing evaluation criteria for media projects, was shaken up.

In the autumn, I saw a flyer on campus for a special lecture by Eric Ries, a young entrepreneur who wanted to talk about using lean methods for high-tech ventures. The lecture was sparsely attended, but was utterly fascinating. Ries, who later released a book titled *The Lean Startup*, had some powerful ideas about product development based on his experience as a software developer and entrepreneur.

In the mid-2000s, Ries cofounded a company called IMVU that intended to capitalize on the instant messaging craze and computer-generated worlds. As chief technical officer, Ries was responsible for overseeing development of a product that let people create three-dimensional characters ("avatars") who could hang out in a computer-generated environment. Critical to IMVU's strategy was building an add-on application that connected the virtual world to instant messaging applications such as AOL Instant Messenger and Yahoo Messenger. The idea was to let users invite their friends to join IMVU.

Ries and his partners perceived a market need, and they designed IMVU as a social platform for the gaming generation. They saw the IM add-on as a clever way to build viral growth. New users could easily invite dozens of friends from their buddy lists. It didn't matter if a user was on AOL or Yahoo Messenger—IMVU could work with them all. The team assumed users would love this feature.

The first version of IMVU ended up taking six months to develop. There were lots of features, from the IM add-on to customization tools for users' avatars. Yet when the product finally launched, it was an utter flop. Practically no one downloaded the software. Only after interviewing test users did the team grasp that most of their initial assumptions about IMVU's target audience were wrong. Testers liked the avatar concept, but they hated the IM connections. Users did not necessarily want to invite their friends—they wanted to use IMVU to make new friends!

Realizing they had misjudged the needs of their prospective customers, Ries and his team went back to the drawing board. Developers ended up throwing away thousands of lines of code to completely rework the product. IMVU eventually settled on a paid virtual world model without IM connections. Growth eventually kicked in, and the company was able to scale up to a real business with millions of dollars in monthly revenue.

Looking back at the experience, Ries acknowledged that IMVU's initial top-down product development process was deeply flawed. The team made a huge leap of faith about the market. They ended up wasting months creating a product that customers did not want. It was a huge mistake that almost killed the company.

IMVU was not alone. "Most of the software projects that are undertaken are never used by anyone," Ries said during his campus lecture. It wasn't just naive startup teams with little market experience wasting time making things that no one wanted. Big corporations made this type of mistake, too, he said.

Ries went on to describe how IMVU recovered after its initial failure. The company started to test its assumptions on a small group of prospective customers *before* engaging in a monumental development effort. Further, once they started building the software, they continued to test assumptions. This entailed creating hypotheses about the business, potential features, and other aspects of IMVU. They then tested their hypotheses, measured the results, and quickly incorporated changes based on what they learned. The cycle would begin anew with a new set of hypotheses, which would generate more insights that could be brought back to the next product iteration.

Ries called this approach *validated learning*, and urged everyone attending his talk to consider it and other aspects of his Lean Startup framework for our own startups. His 2011 book, *The Lean Startup*, articulates the framework in detail. It establishes a connection with some of the same Lean Manufacturing concepts that I had learned about in my supply chain management class, such as eliminating waste and focusing on speed.

While heavy industry and software development appear to have little in common, Ries believes some of the lean methods used by companies such as Toyota can be applied to technology startups. For instance, he values the focus on small batches and continuous improvement, as well as the internal feedback cycles used in the *kanban* production control system to regulate parts procurement and other production processes.

But Ries made one critical change: Whereas Lean Manufacturing feedback cycles are internal, Lean Startup brings the feedback cycle out to the marketplace. Ries insists that startups need to validate product hypotheses from the customers' points of view, not just from the people building the product.

Practically speaking, this means placing pre-release versions of the product— or representations of the product, such as a demonstration video—in front of test customers, and doing so in a way that allows the team to empirically measure the results. Insights gleaned from validated learning can then be brought to the next iteration. This *build-measure-learn* cycle is central to the Lean Startup framework.

What sorts of hypotheses might a startup test? They can involve grand assumptions about the marketplace ("people are interested in buying self-driving cars") or smaller hypotheses about features ("customers need a manual brake pedal to override the car's computer"), design ("customers in North America prefer blue cars"), or marketing ("customers are more likely to sign themselves up to the waiting list if a 2% rebate is offered.")

Let's say the team wants to test the rebate hypothesis. It can create two versions of a website landing page and show it to 200 prospective customers. Half of the customers can be shown the first version, which includes a button that says, "Join waiting list." The other half sees a second version, which features the same button, along with a sentence that promises a 2% rebate to anyone who puts themselves on the waiting list and ends up buying a vehicle.

Join our waiting list – participants who purchase a vehicle will get a 2% rebate! Click the button below to get started:

JOIN WAITING LIST

By comparing the results from the A/B test, the team will better understand the appeal of the rebate. If the results are similar, there is no reason to continue the rebate as prospective customers will sign up at the same rate, regardless of the rebate. If, however, the rebate option has a signup rate that is three times greater, then the team has validated the hypothesis: It makes sense to incorporate the rebate offer into the marketing plan.

The MVP

A vital element of the Lean Startup framework is the minimum viable product (MVP). This is an early version of the product to show a small set of users. It is not necessary to have a perfect product, nor should the team show the MVP to mainstream customers. Rather, the idea is to quickly create a product that has basic functionality for *early adopters* to try out.

An early adopter is a special breed of startup customer. In *The Lean Startup*, Ries writes that early adopters love to see rough versions of a product because they need the product the most and get a thrill from being the first to try it out. They can live with a partial solution, and, according to Ries, will use their imaginations to fill in the rest. They may even be suspicious of the product if it is too polished.

The MVP is not a proof of concept or technical prototype. With an MVP, the team is not trying to determine whether the technology or design actually works. Rather, the MVP is a tool to validate assumptions about customers. Ries writes that an MVP is the fastest way to get a build-measure-learn cycle going. An example cited in *The Lean Startup* is Groupon, the popular "daily deals" website and app. The MVP consisted of a blog and simple PDF coupons. It wasn't much, but it was enough to validate demand for this type of service, which evolved into a digital coupon site.

If the assumptions cannot be validated, Ries says the idea itself may need to be modified, stripped down, or radically changed as part of a *pivot*. The pivot is celebrated in Silicon Valley, and is indeed the story of several successful products including Lyft (which started out as a Web-based carpool service for college students) and Android (which was originally pitched as an operating system for digital cameras).

Product/market fit vs. product/solution fit

Regardless of whether the team pivots or perseveres, the overriding goal is to achieve product/market fit. Marc Andreessen, a co-creator of the Netscape web browser and a well-known Silicon Valley investor, gives the following definition:

"Product/market fit means being in a good market with a product that can satisfy that market."

It sounds so basic. Make something that customers want. Yet countless technology companies—including Ries' company, IMVU—have made the fundamental mistake of building products that customers did *not* want. These companies may achieve product/solution fit, in which a team creates a great product that solves a problem—but it's not a problem that customers care about!

Taken to an extreme, a few companies will spend years trying to find customers for such products, but eventually will be forced to abandon the effort. Research conducted by CB Insights found that the number one reason startups fail is because there is no market need.

This issue has also tripped up large, established companies. In the early 2010s, high-definition 3D television sets were supposed to be the next big thing in consumer electronics. Asian manufacturers spent billions developing a technology that could display 3D programs in owners' living rooms. They assumed audiences wanted a more immersive television experience than two-dimensional HD sets could provide. Crucially, companies including Panasonic, Samsung, Sony, and Philips intended to sell 3D sets with higher profit margins, as the market for standard HD televisions was being flooded by low-end Chinese and Taiwanese competitors.

The companies worked out standards, enlisted partners in Hollywood and elsewhere to develop 3D programming, and built out production lines to handle the anticipated flood of orders. A colossal marketing campaign started, promising an incredible 3D experience right in people's homes.

But the massive flood of orders never materialized. Audiences were not interested in 3D television. The sets were too expensive. The programming was not compelling. And, there were technical requirements that did not go over

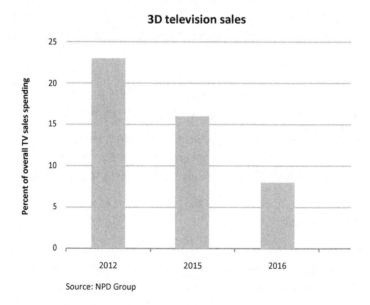

3D television sales

Source: NPD Group

well—viewers had to wear glasses and/or view the set at a certain angle. Some viewers even reported headaches from watching 3D programs.

Demand for 3D sets languished. While 3D TV sales accounted for just over 20% of overall TV purchases in 2012, four years later just 8% of overall TV sales were made up of 3D sets.

In other words, the high-end manufacturers had misread the market. They had achieved a product/solution fit, but failed to find product/market fit. The manufacturers were so caught up with their vision that it took years of lackluster sales before they realized most people simply did not care about 3D television. In early 2017, several major manufacturers announced they were stopping production of 3D sets.

A lean approach to media?

Ries had framed Lean Startup for software and technology ventures, but I realized some of the things he was saying about product development, feedback cycles, and speed could have implications for media as well.

I had seen it with my own eyes. Print content, websites, video, and other media could be developed using lean methods, and had many positive attributes. They were cheaper to produce. User feedback loops started sooner. They made it to market more quickly. Such projects also tended to be more fun for creators to work on.

Conversely, media that took the "chubby" approach—large teams, top-down directives, planning by committee, depending on secrecy and hype to build audience interest—tended to encounter problems. They required more staff and budget commitments, took a long time to complete, and more often than not led to mediocrity ... or expensive failures.

I considered many examples from my own career. One website redevelopment project I had taken part in involved the boss gathering all the heavy hitters in a conference room to hash out his vision. We then spent more than a year developing and tweaking the website in secret. Designed by a committee, the project was loaded with features, yet had nothing to make it stand out from what was already available. After it launched, audiences didn't care.

I decided to look more deeply into Lean Startup. The framework had worked for IMVU and other companies cited by Ries, including Dropbox and Intuit. Just as Lean Production represented a new approach to manufacturing, Lean Startup represented a different approach to product development in technology startups. Was there a place for media in the lean frameworks?

Takeaways

- Lean Manufacturing focuses on managing limited resources and supplier relationships to increase efficiency.

- Lean Startup lays out an iterative product development process based on understanding customers.

- The MVP is not a proof of concept or technical prototype, but rather an early version of the product to show a small set of early adopters to validate assumptions.

- Many media companies take a "chubby" approach to production and marketing, assigning a big team to work on a project in secret and then trying to build hype around the launch to create blockbuster success.

2

A new media world

To understand the impetus for creating a new framework for media, it helps to understand the conflagration that has engulfed the media industry in recent decades. At the beginning of this book, I described my experience navigating the tumultuous media landscape of the 1990s and 2000s. Disruptive change started much earlier, beginning with the introduction of relatively inexpensive computers and software tools in the 1970s and early 1980s.

This first wave of digital technologies had a widespread impact upon media production. Instead of using a typewriter to prepare an article or manuscript, a new generation of journalists, authors, and editors began using PCs. In Hollywood, visual effects designers and animators migrated from film-based technologies, costumes, and miniature models to digital animation and computer-generated imagery (CGI). Musicians and recording engineers experimented with digital tools such as samplers and MIDI, a technical standard for electronic instruments.

Concurrently, videogames such as Pong, Space Invaders, and simple home console games were the first true digital media experiences for large swathes of the population. While other consumer media experiences still depended on older analog formats such as LPs and magnetic tape, they were steadily replaced by digital technologies such as the compact disc and DVD.

In the 1990s, the pace of disruption accelerated. Sophisticated software began to infiltrate more areas of production and distribution. The World Wide Web and email moved from academic labs to mainstream use. Electronics also became more advanced. It wasn't enough to have a single-feature device, such as a videogame console or a CD player. Gadgets began to sprout more features and functions, such as network capabilities and specialized apps. For instance, the humble mobile phone was a calls-only device in 1990. Ten years later, phones came with address books and simple games. By 2010, most new phones had apps to play video and audio, connect with friends, and integrate with sophisticated calendaring systems. Smartphone penetration has grown steadily since then, with levels in the U.S. currently above 75%.

Smartphone ownership, 2011-2017

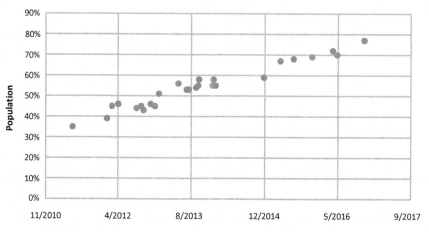

Source: Pew Research Center

By the late 1990s, the media industry began to accept that digital technologies would have a far-reaching impact on nearly every aspect of making, distributing, consuming, and monetizing media. Audiences were splintering, and media creators were contending with a slew of new business models. Technology platforms were taking the world by storm. Some platforms, such as the World Wide Web, were open for anyone to use and experiment with. Others were controlled by software and hardware companies who put their own needs and profits ahead of the creators and brands who used them. It could be frustrating trying to chart a course through the choppy seas of change, but there was no going back. Indeed, there was an ominous sense that there would be winners and losers—and the losers were more likely to be the established players than the upstarts.

Within the media industry, different sectors experienced different dynamics when it came to technology, platforms, business models, and audience behavior. While there were parallels between certain sectors, there were often profound differences.

Tremors in the music industry

The music industry was the first to experience the pain. The advent of digital recording technologies and the compact disc had been welcome advances, and helped generate record profits in the 1990s. Musicians also appreciated the ability to use websites, email newsletters, and nascent social networks to connect directly with audiences, bypassing traditional publicity and marketing channels.

The music industry had a large degree of control over production technologies and their own digital marketing channels. The Internet—a global, decentralized communication network—was another story. It was vast, disorganized, and largely unregulated, yet audiences loved it.

The Internet was optimized for the transfer of digital information, including email, text, and images. The network could also be used to transfer digital files, such as music encoded with the mp3 digital compression standard. Websites began to pop up, offering illegal mp3 file downloads. When someone downloaded an mp3 file containing one of his or her favorite songs, the artist and the record label received no compensation.

That was bad enough, but by the end of the decade, major labels, lawyers, and lobbyists were scrambling to deal with the appearance of new file-sharing applications. After installing Napster and similar applications on a PC, audiences could easily download hundreds or even thousands of pirated mp3 music files for free. Musicians rarely inserted themselves into the fray—those who did often found themselves at the receiving end of Internet-driven viral anger. The heavy metal band Metallica was slammed by its own fans when it demanded they stop using file-sharing services.

A second blow came a few years later with Apple's introduction of a new digital music ecosystem. It included a platform for purchasing songs—iTunes—and a portable device for playing songs, the iPod. It was convenient and well-designed.

Apple also instituted another innovation: It allowed audiences to purchase individual songs for an Apple-mandated price of 99 cents. This may not seem important, but it allowed consumers to purchase just the songs they liked, instead of having to buy the entire album.

CD sales were hammered. As profits fell, labels were forced to downsize and re-evaluate business models. But just as the industry was coming to terms with the Apple ecosystem, a new threat emerged in the form of streaming music platforms. Instead of downloading digital copies of songs to PCs or mobile devices, services like Pandora and Spotify establish a live digital connection to deliver music to listeners. They offer libraries containing millions of songs, as well as features that let audiences organize playlists or discover new music. Free versions of the applications force audiences to view or listen to advertisements. A small percentage of listeners opt to pay for monthly subscriptions that eliminate the ads and activate other features, such as the ability to download songs to mobile devices or access to curated or algorithmically generated playlists.

Streaming services have exploded. From 2014 to 2016, the number of streams delivered to listeners more than doubled. If the trend continues, U.S. audiences will listen to more than a half-trillion music streams annually.

Growth of U.S. on-demand music streaming

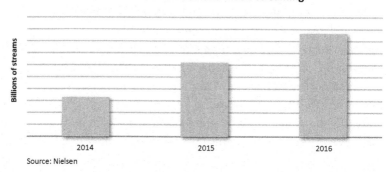

Source: Nielsen

The streaming services have further eroded the business of selling music. Twenty-five years ago, a dedicated music fan might have spent several hundred dollars per year on new albums. Now it's possible for the same fan to have a nearly unlimited supply of music for $10 per month or even less if he or she uses free streaming services, YouTube, and other Internet sources.

The only creators who do well in the era of streaming music are those musicians who have the muscle to cut special deals or can generate massive scale. Everyone else gets crumbs. In 2014, Bette Midler reported earning just $114 on more than 4 million "plays" on Pandora. Taylor Swift, a singer who is able to achieve massive scale, yanked her music (with her label's blessing) from Spotify in 2014, complaining that the service was not fairly compensating her or other artists. (Several years later, Swift and her music label worked out a deal to bring her albums back to Spotify.)

As a result of the bottom falling out of the market for recorded music, musicians are now turning to other sources of revenue. Those with big enough followings can attract audiences to live performances. Others try to license music for film, television, and advertising. Independent musicians leverage crowdsourcing services to fund tours or new studio recordings.

Challenges to the film and broadcasting industries

Like the music industry, the film industry was paranoid about the potential for online piracy to eat into profits. But Hollywood was better prepared. After experiencing videotape piracy in the 80s, the film industry insisted new digital formats such as DVDs contain technologies to thwart piracy and even casual copying. Later, when file-sharing services appeared, piracy of films and television programs was relatively limited compared to recorded music files. This was partially due to technical constraints—most home users did not have the Internet bandwidth, storage capacity, or the patience to download gigantic video files. Hollywood also put legal pressure on Internet service providers, hosting services, and website operators to remove pirated files and download services.

When Netflix morphed from a DVD-delivery service to an inexpensive sub-scription-based streaming service in the mid-2000s, the film industry (and its cable TV allies) adopted a scarcity strategy, strictly limiting licensing of hit movies and TV shows to streaming services. If audiences wanted to stream movies onto their new large-screen LCD TVs, then they would be stuck watching reruns and second-rate films from previous decades, along with documentaries, foreign-language films, and whatever low-budget indie films Netflix managed to license. If audiences wanted the hits, they would have to come to theaters, buy DVDs, or pay for an expensive cable TV package.

Hollywood may have assumed it had a strategy to trump Netflix. But it did not anticipate trends in audience behavior or the ingenuity of digital compet-itors. Subscribers loved the convenience and low prices of Netflix and other streaming services, such as Hulu and Amazon Video.

Millions more turned to free Internet videos on YouTube and elsewhere. Though the quality of free clips did not come close to professionally pro-duced video, they were still entertaining and informative. Content included everything from homemade cat videos to comedy shorts and dramas created by up-and-coming young producers using inexpensive video cameras and PC-based editing software. There were many other types of videos, including old variety shows, sporting events, and even screencasts of people playing (and commenting on) video games.

The streaming companies were also able to form alliances with Viacom and other content owners who wanted cash or exposure. The agreements allowed Netflix to stream more popular shows and recent hits, which helped attract and retain subscribers. In addition, by the early teens, Netflix and Amazon started to develop their own programming. It was an expensive and risky strategy, but it paid off with exclusive hits such as *Orange Is The New Black* and *Man In The High Castle*.

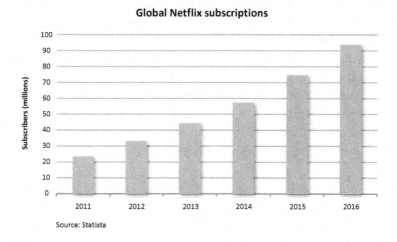

Global Netflix subscriptions

Source: Statista

As global Netflix subscriptions tripled from 2011 to 2016, broadcasters saw their power erode. For decades, radio and television stations and large national networks such as ABC, NBC, and CBS controlled what Americans heard and saw. A famous DJ or variety show could make or break a new band or a new brand. A powerful news anchor or talk show host could change public opinion. Comedies, dramas, soap operas, sitcoms, game shows, and news shows generated billions of dollars in profit every year for the networks and local affiliates.

Cable television began to erode the power of broadcasters beginning in the 1980s. But at least broadcasters could work with the cable industry, through syndication and other deals. With the new crop of digital platforms? Not so much. The advent of the Internet in the 1990s and the popularity of gadgets like the iPod and digital video recorders in the early 2000s began to upend the broadcast model. Audiences now had alternatives. They no longer needed late-night TV hosts, shock jocks, news directors, or programming executives to keep themselves entertained and informed. YouTube, Netflix, and video streaming platforms accelerated the trend in television, while music streaming services further eroded the power of radio. Nowadays, few TV hosts, DJs, or news anchors are making or breaking new artists or changing national attitudes. More often than not, audiences can be swayed by a viral video, Internet meme, a popular Spotify playlist, or powerful endorsements created by performers and promoted by friends on social networks.

The migration of broadcast audiences to new digital platforms has caused advertising profits to wither. The fewer eyeballs watching a TV program or listening to a radio show, the less the station or network can charge advertisers to show a 30-second commercial. But that's not the only thing that's contributing to shrinking broadcast revenue. Companies that want to show their wares or market their services not only have new mediums and platforms to turn to, but they also have access to data that lets them better target ads and measure the results. Using online or mobile ad networks, a company can pay a precise amount of money to achieve an impression, click, or lead. Facebook's ad platform even lets advertisers select micro-targeted demographic groups (for instance, Chicago residents 18 and over owning a late-model Android phone) to allow for focused campaigns. The following graphic shows the performance of a Facebook ad campaign, breaking out the number of impressions and clicks on the advertisement by age and gender:

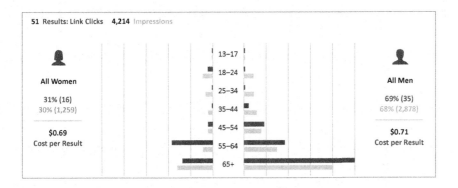

By comparison, broadcast media is notoriously difficult to measure. Most ratings are based on sampling techniques and statistical extrapolations. Targeting is imprecise, and tying results to specific campaigns is more an art than a science. Because digital campaigns are easier to quantify, companies are assigning ever-larger portions of their marketing dollars to online and mobile advertising, while reducing broadcast expenditures.

Disruption in print, struggles in new digital formats

Magazines and newspapers have been hammered by shifting audience preferences and a slew of new competitors, including specialty apps, blogs, and powerhouse personalities on social media. Print advertising, which once supported large editorial staffs and fancy downtown headquarters, has been hammered by digital alternatives. One website—Craigslist—is largely responsible for eviscerating the newspaper classifieds market. According to the News Media Alliance, an industry trade group, advertising in national brands, retail, classified, and other categories generated $48.7 billion in the United States in 2000. Ten years later, the figure dropped to $22.8 billion.

Newspaper advertising revenue, 1950-2010

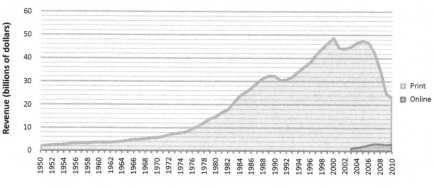

Source: News Media Alliance

Newspaper and magazine publishers have tried to stay relevant to both readers and advertisers by launching their own websites and apps. It has been an uphill battle. There are simply too many free or low-cost alternatives clamoring for people's attention.

Digital publishers can now leverage cheaper and easier-to-configure content management systems, cloud hosting, shopping carts, and social media plugins to get a new site off the ground. Traditional publishers can leverage these technologies as well, but they also have to support expensive legacy production and distribution costs, such as printing plants and home delivery. In effect, someone working out of his or her bedroom can launch a new website and compete with established publishing brands at a much lower cost.

This is exactly what happened in the tech media space, where I used to work. In the late 1990s, I remember senior executives giving a slideshow about the competition, which at the time consisted of two other established print publishers. Ten years later, there were dozens of competitors, most of them online. They included TechCrunch, a Silicon Valley news site started in 2005 by lawyer Michael Arrington using off-the-shelf blog software. By the time I left IDG, TechCrunch was going head-to-head with our events business, and built a database of technology investments that was closely followed in Silicon Valley. TechCrunch was eventually acquired by AOL, and is still going strong today.

However, new online publishers are contending with the problem of monetizing their output. Audiences expect news and blogs to be free. Subscription plans are nonstarters for most readers, except for highly specialized sites with unique content (think the *Financial Times* or *Wall Street Journal*). Audiences also don't like to click on advertisements, with some going so far as to install special ad-blocking software on their phones, tablets, and computers.

There is also the issue of a practically unlimited supply of web pages, app screens, and social media feeds. This generally depresses the value of sites' inventories, although Google and social media sites can attract higher prices for targeted keywords or demographic groups. For most online publishers, the only way to achieve profit by selling advertisements is through massive scale, offering specialized marketing programs to advertising partners, or leveraging affiliate programs that pay money to publishers who deliver paying customers to retailers such as Amazon. Major media outlets are also inserting videos, articles, and other content directly into products controlled by major technology platforms, such as Facebook and Apple.

Online publishing has also enabled a wave of disintermediation that has undercut the news media. Prior to the invention of the World Wide Web, companies, politicians, organizations, and other entities depended on traditional media outlets to reach the public. Starting in the mid-1990s, they realized they could bypass the gatekeepers, and connect directly with consumers.

Brand websites began to proliferate. At first, they contained little more than contact information, basic product details, and support resources. Over time, they began to incorporate blogs, social media features, video, and specialized content designed to attract customers and build influence. There is now an emerging "content marketing" industry utilized by corporations and other organizations, often employing the same writers and editors who used to cover them in the news media!

Publishers of video games and console manufacturers started out with blocky 2D titles in the late 1970s and early 1980s. By 2000, consoles and PC hardware could support richly detailed 3D games as well as networked play. Gaming evolved into a multibillion dollar industry, on par with the movie and music businesses. But competition was fierce, with console manufacturers vying for supremacy and game studios vying to get noticed. New platforms, features, and fads would come and go every few years. In 2005, the Nintendo Wii was the breakout console product. A few years later, console gamers rallied around the powerful Sony PlayStation and Microsoft Xbox systems. Meanwhile, social and mobile gaming appeared on the scene, attracting new audiences and convincing some people to abandon consoles.

One of the oldest forms of mass media, books, evolved differently. Because most people don't like to read novels on computer monitors, the book industry was somewhat insulated from the digital revolution upending newspapers and magazines. However, the Internet had a profound impact on retail. The early upstart was Amazon, which transformed the sale of books starting in the 1990s.

At first, online retailing was more of a threat to book merchants than publishers. Amazon was not satisfied with only taking market share from book retailers, though. Founder Jeff Bezos had targeted one of the most inefficient and vulnerable media sectors, and continued his assault on the industry with a host of new services and platforms. They included the Kindle, a portable e-reader that let readers download ebooks.

Simultaneously, Amazon created or bought services such as Kindle Direct Publishing (an ebook publishing service) and Createspace (a print-on-demand paperback service) that let independent authors publish books on their own. This made it possible for authors to bypass traditional publishers and distributors, and sell ebooks and paperbacks to Amazon's hundreds of millions of customers (with Amazon taking a cut, naturally). Amazon has used its marketplace dominance to force ebook prices lower and marginalize competitors in the United States and elsewhere.

Amazon's impact on the book industry cannot be overstated. In the 1990s, the U.S. book industry published tens of thousands of titles annually, as measured by the number of unique ISBN numbers (an international standard for book registration) issued to publishers. Now, more than one million ISBN numbers are issued every year in the U.S. for both print and ebook formats, with many of them used by independent or self-published authors.

Despite these innovations, ebook sales have plateaued in recent years. While print book sales are holding steady, the number of sales channels has dropped as large bookstore chains have failed and big box stores devote less shelf space to books. Large publishing companies have responded by becoming more risk-averse, preferring books written by celebrities or authors with large social media followings. Such titles may have more marketing potential, but this approach may be neglecting important works that may also resonate with audiences.

Embracing new production tools

The digital revolution hasn't all been doom and gloom. While disruption has shaken up marketplaces, the shift to digital production tools has positively impacted the media industry in numerous ways. Digital technologies have also made it possible to apply lean methods to media production.

At the heart of the digital production trend is the development of computer-based standards, software, and equipment for media content. Audio or video used to be recorded on magnetic tape. This information can now be stored as bits on hard drives, flash memory, or cloud servers. Further, ancient mechanical processes—a spool wrapped with celluloid travelling in front of a bright light, or ink-covered iron letters pressed against paper—have been replaced with software and screens.

Those of us whose careers started in the 20th century have witnessed a massive transition from expensive analog technologies to cheaper and more efficient digital replacements. Journalists of a certain age will remember writing articles on a typewriter and taking photographs with an SLR film camera, and developing the film in a darkroom reeking of chemicals. In the music industry, professional recording studios once used 2-inch magnetic tapes to simultaneously record 24 tracks of audio. Film people may remember the Steenbeck, a monstrous contraption with spindles, pulleys, and a small backlit screen that was used to edit film and the accompanying audio.

These technologies seem backwards or quaint now. Not only are the digital replacements cheaper, but they are also easier to use and have new capabilities. Consider the equipment I used in the mid-1990s to edit broadcast news clips. The setup consisted of a Sony CRT monitor, two heavy BetaCam recorders, and ¾-inch videotapes that were as large as a hardcover novel. The rig must have weighed close to 100 pounds, and required a dolly to move around the studio. Nowadays, it is possible to shoot HD video on a smartphone, and make sophisticated edits using a cheap app, and immediately post the results to YouTube!

The new tools are utterly liberating. They allow creators to be more efficient at what they do. They also let creators produce media for audiences and channels that did not even exist until recently.

People who love to create media have largely embraced new production technologies. Sure, there are a few holdouts who treasure old production processes, or purists who insist that analog media is qualitatively better. But by and large, no one laments the passing of typewriters, film cameras, darkrooms, tape decks, or splicing tools. The replacement technologies enable the creation of better media.

The false allure of chubby media

Across the globe, creators have turned to digital technologies to produce their work. Media outlets use digital platforms to distribute their content. Audiences now depend on digital devices to engage with media. It's a world of bits and bytes, ones and zeroes, and likes and shares.

Despite the changes in the toolsets, platforms, and business models, one thing has remained constant for creators: Production usually takes place in secret, largely disconnected from audiences they are trying to inform or entertain.

This is a legacy of the old ways of producing media, in which creators were cloistered in their workshops and studios, keeping their ideas under wraps while their works were perfected for launch. This approach persists today. There may be extensive approvals involved, as various managers, stakeholders, and investors are brought in to give their feedback or sign off on a particular element. Meanwhile, marketing teams center their efforts around making as big a splash as possible on the launch date, which means arranging for advance media coverage and coordinating promotional campaigns.

Conceptually, the chubby media workflow looks something like this:

The problem with this approach is the people behind the production don't know what audiences will think until *after* the launch. They may not even know who their audiences are!

It's tempting to suppose the same elements the creative team thinks are special—the set design for the period film drama, the jokes in the sitcom script, the percussion on a new dance song, the quirky personality of the prime-time news anchor—will resonate with audiences. These days, there is so much information available about audiences and trends, that some self-serving data point can usually be trotted out to support the vision. Creators may spend months or even years getting their masterpieces ready. If the chubby launch is successful and audiences love it, that's great. The demanding work will have been worth it.

But what if it flops? What if the team put its heart and soul into making a new website, video, album, or game, and it fails to connect with audiences after the launch? This is the reality of most new media projects.

Consider the movie industry. In Hollywood, 90% of film projects never make it out of development. Further, there is no guarantee of success for the films that do end up getting released. According to one estimate, more than 50% of blockbuster films are failures.

Every year, there seems to be one epic flop that outdoes them all. In 2013, it was the star-studded remake of *The Lone Ranger* (reported loss: $42-$125 million). The following year, *Legends of Oz: Dorothy's Return* reportedly cost more than $80 million to make and grossed only $20 million. The table below shows some of the all-time worst Hollywood flops, with films such as *The Adventures of Pluto Nash* and *Heaven's Gate* grossing a fraction of backers' investments. (Investments are in millions.)

Title	Year	Studio	Investment	Worldwide gross
Legends of Oz: Dorothy's Return	2014	Clarius	$83	$20
Lone Ranger	2013	Disney	$302	$260
Mars Needs Moms	2011	Disney	$200	$39
Gigli	2003	Sony	$54	$7
The Adventures of Pluto Nash	2002	Warner Bros.	$100	$7
Town & Country	2001	New Line	$90	$10
Battlefield Earth	2000	Warner Bros.	$74	$22
The Postman	1997	Warner Bros.	$100	$18
Cutthroat Island	1995	MGM/Carolco	$100	$10
Hudson Hawk	1991	Columbia TriStar	$60	$17
Heaven's Gate	1980	United Artist	$45	$3
Cleopatra	1963	20th Century Fox	$44	$26

Sources: Hollywood Reporter, The Numbers

Of course, it's possible to find a silver lining in failed launches. Creators can legitimately cite failure as a learning experience. Sometimes it may even be possible to salvage something out of the wreckage—an idea, a character, a theme, or a melody that can be repurposed later on.

But let's be honest: Does a "learning experience" really require wasting months or even years of time, effort, and money? Wouldn't it be better to have a learning experience that takes only a few weeks or months to realize, and occurs *before* something crashes and burns in public?

Imagine if we knew what audiences liked and didn't like about a particular media work while it was still being produced, and creative teams were able to make substantive improvements in response to feedback throughout the development phase. It would be a game-changer for many media organizations. This is what the Lean Media framework strives to do. It's not hard; successful, creative people often start out with such techniques (but are generally unaware they are using a lean framework). Many musicians instinctively know the importance of audience feedback to improving songs and live performances. As Bruno Mars noted in a CBS interview about his early years as a performer, "If the audience wasn't freaking out, you're not doing it right."

We will take a look at some examples in the chapters that follow, and outline the key elements of the Lean Media framework.

Takeaways

- While digital media technologies have upended traditional business models, they have also reduced production costs and enabled new modes of distribution.

- Technology platforms controlled by Amazon, Facebook, and others have gained control and power over the media industry at the expense of creators, publishers, and retailers.

- The traditional "chubby" approach to media production and marketing leads to a high failure rate.

3

Finding a lean fit for media content

As described in the Introduction, I was introduced to Lean Manufacturing through a business school class on supply chain management. Not long after, I learned how Eric Ries, the author of *The Lean Startup*, brought Lean Manufacturing concepts into the realm of iterative product development at tech startups. Ries' Lean Startup methodology was compelling to me at the time, especially when I considered the similarities between his experience at IMVU and some of the media development projects I had worked on over the years.

But is Lean Startup a good fit for teams creating media? After listening to Ries' talk and reading *The Lean Startup*, it became clear to me that certain aspects of the framework don't jive with the way my industry works:

- The "scientific approach" to measuring feedback neglects important qualitative elements of media.

- The MVP/early adopter concept might work for a physical product or paid business service with a well-defined market, but not necessarily for media that depends on amorphous emotional and aesthetic qualities and constantly shifting audience tastes.

- Several practices outlined in Ries' book have little relevance to new media or media ventures, and can even lead to negative outcomes.

On this last point, consider *innovation accounting*, a metrics-driven system for startups to measure progress, set milestones, make product decisions, and target certain customer segments. While innovation accounting might be useful to founders of a software company or a producer of mechanical widgets, it seems too rigid for most media ventures, and could potentially constrain the creativity of the team.

Another idea that can be eliminated is the *Five Whys* process for identifying the root cause of a production problem. Ries adapted Five Whys from a Lean Manufacturing methodology developed by Taiichi Ohno, the legendary Toyota engineer behind the Toyota Production System. While it has some relevance for those media that required extensive engineering, such as a video game or website, I anticipated it could be counterproductive for teams working on print media, music, advertising, or video. A problem with the production of a media work can sometimes be tied to a faulty process or a broken tool. However, many "problems" actually relate to creative and personality differences. Such issues are highly subjective and are resistant to a troubleshooting process originally developed for heavy industry.

In addition, creative friction among people making media often leads to brilliance. This may seem strange to outsiders—how can a team that appears hopelessly dysfunctional get anything done? Nevertheless, team members often find ways to strike a balance or form some sort of truce that allows a project to move forward.

In 1993, iD Software released DOOM, a groundbreaking combat video game that transformed the PC game industry. Yet the team of highly talented designers and programmers who made DOOM was riven by conflict. Then there's the Lennon/McCartney dynamic in The Beatles, which was beset by rivalry and resentment, yet managed to create some of the most incredible songs of the 20th century.

There are many more examples, ranging from the brilliant yet eccentric writer who can never meet editors' deadlines, to the tyrannical film director who browbeats everyone on the set but creates an Oscar-worthy film. I fear that introducing Five Whys as a way to solve problems in a media setting may end up undermining key people, or sabotaging creative tension. It does not make much sense to bring it into a media organization.

Media is not like other products

In addition to team dynamics, there is also the issue of the product itself. Consider a tech startup that is trying to make a better light bulb, exercise tracker, or software-as-a-service targeting the insurance industry. Under Lean Startup, the firm has to validate assumptions, show MVPs to early adopters, test hypotheses, and learn from the results. Startups are supposed to take a scientific approach in how they measure feedback about the product they are working on, and act upon it to improve the next iteration of the product. The Build-Measure-Learn feedback cycle, honed by quantitively derived conclusions about customers' needs, lies at the heart of Lean Startup. The ultimate goal of the framework? To achieve product-market fit, and make a sustainable business.

Media people march to the beat of a different drum. We don't make light bulbs or exercise trackers. We have no interest in signing up corporate clients for software-as-a-service contracts. I've never heard of anyone involved in a creative media venture asking about the "value proposition" for customers or the timetable for achieving product-market fit.

That's not to say a publisher or studio or artist manager doesn't care about the business of media. Of course someone will need to figure out a way to generate revenue or otherwise support the underlying mission of the organization. But for the people creating the actual media experience, there are non-business motives that dominate their work.

Media creators have a profound desire to make media that has unique creative, aesthetic, or artistic value. They feel great personal satisfaction in bringing their creations to the world and seeing others appreciate what they have built. They strive to make something that will cause people to laugh, cry, dance, clap, gain a sense of excitement or outrage or desire, or better understand the world around them. The ultimate achievement: releasing something meaningful that has a lasting impact on society for years or even decades to come, and influences other creators in the future.

For some, participating in the creation of media is a form of self-expression. Others revel in the collaborative process of working with a talented team to create something wonderful. Nearly all are driven to do what they do, whether it is taking to the stage, composing a new song, spending all night editing a book, or rising at 5 am to take photographs in the early morning light. Many will work on media even if there is little or no monetary return.

If you have ever created media, whether it's a neighborhood blog or a blockbuster film, you know what I am talking about. This creative dimension is core to our identities. We feel compelled to make media, and strive to be great at what we do.

Of course, people making light bulbs or cars or software-as-a-service can be creative, too. However, the creativity manifests itself differently. The engineer at a lighting startup may figure out a unique method to make more efficient light bulbs using special composite materials. An industrial design group may come up with a space-saving design for a car's interior. A programmer may find a brilliant approach to simplifying a software process. The sales team may devise a new partnership that increases their employer's customer base. The CEO and her HR chief may come up with an innovative benefit that helps her company recruit better people. While these examples all reflect creativity, it's a different type of creativity than in the media world.

There are other differences between media ventures and technology startups. A startup is closely aligned to business goals, which are almost always focused on creating products, services, or something else that can be sold and scaled to achieve maximum profit. The product or service could end up changing the world, or may result in some incredible technological breakthrough or design idea. In some cases, the startup may have some noble mission—although over time it may be watered down by business considerations. Ultimately, the success of most tech ventures comes back to selling something and making money.

For media creators, feelings of success come from the act of creating something great, and the audience appreciation and peer recognition that follow. Success may also be correlated with sales, particularly for large, profit-oriented media businesses. But few creators say money is the primary motivation behind great media.

The differing natures of tech startups and media ventures are also reflected in the people who end up using the respective products. Startups have customers and users with specific needs (e.g., an energy-efficient light bulb or a sophisticated communications app) and/or an expectation that they are getting something with tangible value in exchange for handing over their money. This is true even of products that have a deep design component, such as high-end mobile phones, jewelry, and sports cars. The design and brand may attract customers and create bonds with owners, but such products also serve practical needs.

Among consumers of media, no one "needs" a movie, news subscription, or video game like they need a light bulb or a software application. There is certainly value to the audiences, but it is derived from visceral, intangible qualities of the experience such as excitement, pleasure, imagination, humor, understanding, and discovery.

The attachment to media can at times be so strong that an audience member will stay up all night binge-watching a TV series or finishing a novel. The same person will come back for more when the next season is released on Netflix or the author finishes another book in the series. That type of bond is seldom replicated when he or she buys a light bulb or signs up for an online software utility. Even when strong design elements are present in a product and manage to stir customers' aesthetic sensibilities, it's the underlying functionality and value that will seal the deal and keep customers coming back for more.

The following diagram plots various types of media on the axes of intangible vs. practical needs and physical vs. non-physical characteristics. Few non-media products stray far into the intangible realm. When they do, they typically have strong practical qualities as well, or have a high degree of tangible value. A new sports car may have a beautiful exterior design and neat software features, but it also serves a very practical purpose of transporting occupants from point A to point B. Smartphones and their operating systems may be aesthetically pleasing to behold and operate, but they also help their owners communicate with other people and perform other practical functions. Social networks are not just about posting vacation photos—they serve an important human need to stay connected with family, friends, and coworkers.

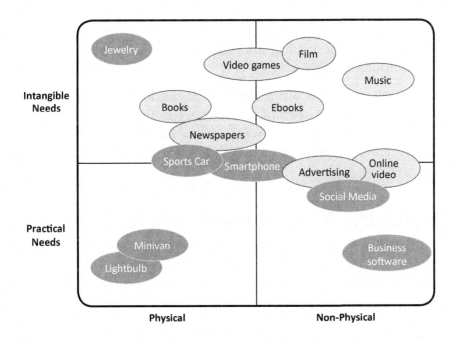

The problem with MVPs

A core element of Lean Startup is the minimum viable product. The idea of using an MVP to validate assumptions has a lot of merit, but it is not universally accepted. Mentioning "MVP" in certain industry circles is likely to generate eye rolls or groans. The tech landscape is littered with the husks of barely functional prototypes billed as "MVPs" that never should have been presented to customers, such as a software-as-a-service product that keeps throwing error messages, or the gadget that trails wires from its casing and makes a loud buzzing sound when turned on. Something that is too basic or nonfunctional is unlikely to generate much useful feedback, even among customers who are receptive to seeing early prototypes.

When it comes to media, there are additional considerations. Audiences are sensitive to unfinished works such as an incomplete song or a video game that only goes up to level 2. But they can become positively uncomfortable if the early version is littered with the scaffolding required to produce the media. Consider the following examples:

- An early manuscript by a popular novelist covered with annotations, copy editors' marks, and scratched-out words.

- A website with broken navigation and misplaced graphic design elements.

- The demo version of a song featuring a rhythmic clacking of a metronome dominating the mix.

These elements will be distracting to test audiences, and will make it hard for them to give useful feedback. It may even turn them against the media, either by casting a negative pall over the production or revealing the tricks of the trade in ways that undermine the suspension of disbelief that is required for so many formats.

Data doesn't tell the whole story for media

One of the biggest issues that prevented me from regarding Lean Startup as a suitable tool for media ventures was the relentless focus on quantitative metrics. According to Ries, validated learning has to be derived via a scientific approach based upon empirical data.

Media ventures have used data to understand audiences and business prospects going back to Gutenberg's time. Today, an incredible array of sophisticated sales, usage, and engagement data is available to media ventures both small and large. However, quantitative data does not tell the whole story. This information has to live side by side with vital intangible qualities, too. Even the most hard-nosed broadcast ratings analyst or web traffic guru understands that good numbers depend on great media. The media has to be magical to make the numbers soar.

During the development process, when creators and producers are striving to make that magic happen, critical attention will be focused on charisma, language, quality, uniqueness, timing, energy, emotional connections, and other elements that are difficult to measure. Numbers can certainly help creative teams understand their audiences and make decisions. But a media team guided solely by quantitative data is bound to overlook crucial intangibles, and even lead teams down false paths. When the creative magic takes a backseat to business or marketing metrics, the end result tends to be uninspiring "me too" media that fails to impress audiences.

According to Don Daglow, a veteran video game executive, "Creative teams without vision who want the audience to lead them to revenue are just following the cow around the pasture." In his view, the team must start with a clear creative vision of what they are planning and why it will work.

In the late 2000s, the poster child for metrics-driven media was Zynga. The gaming company enjoyed early success on mobile and social platforms with games like FarmVille and Mafia Wars. By 2010, it had 360 million monthly active users, and the following year the company launched an initial public stock offering on the Nasdaq stock exchange, raising a billion dollars. The company was on a roll, and for a while it seemed to have a formula that allowed it to make hit game after hit game.

The company's co-founder and CEO, Mark Pincus, was obsessed with metrics, which infused the company's culture. In a 2011 *Wall Street Journal* article, one executive described Zynga as "an analytics company masquerading as a games company." Zynga's development teams followed a rigid formula to making games. Employees made countless decisions based on metrics derived from a powerful in-house analytical engine that tracked specific user actions, such as vitality, retention, and revenue per user. The company was dominated by analysts, product managers, engineers, and executives who trusted numbers more than their guts. Designers and other creative types took a back seat.

While Farmville and Mafia Wars were hot, everyone thought that Zynga's hit-making formula was a stroke of brilliance. But then the company started to falter. By the early teens, growth had slowed, and the company's stock price began to slide. It wasn't just because the social and mobile marketplaces were changing. The titles developed in-house by Zynga tended to be uninspiring copies of past hits (CastleVille, FishVille, ChefVille and various Mafia Wars permutations), or twists on existing genres, such as poker and word scrambles. Zynga tried to right the ship with the acquisition of several up-and-coming game studios. But it was forced to lay off hundreds of workers and restructure its operations in 2013 and 2015. Revenue plateaued.

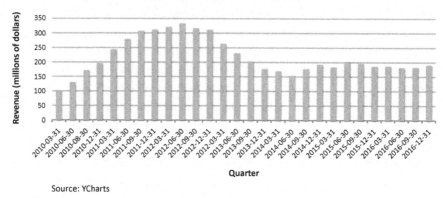

Zynga quarterly revenue, 2010-2016

Source: YCharts

There are several takeaways from Zynga's experience with data-driven media development:

1. **Quantitative feedback does not tell the whole story about why audiences like or dislike media.** Quantitative data can reveal audience ratings, conversion rates, time spent on site, bounce rates, social shares, revenue per user, and ratings on a five-star scale. Such data can certainly inform creators. But quantitative feedback is not as useful when it comes to gaining nuanced insights into why someone left the website after 10 seconds, shared the video clip with a specific group of friends on a social media network, or decided to give a four-star rating for a new movie instead of five stars.

2. **There is a danger in relying too heavily on data in a fast-changing field with fickle audiences such as gaming or music.** In the media industry, data tends to highlight past successes rather than pointing the way to future trends. One of Zynga's most well-known acquisitions was Draw Something, which it acquired (along with mobile app developer OMGPOP) for a reported $183 million in 2012. This occurred after Draw Something had racked up impressive adoption and usage statistics. After the acquisition was complete, audience preferences changed. Zynga's analytical teams and marketing expertise were unable to anticipate the shift or change audience's minds. In 2013, Zynga was forced to write down nearly half of what it had paid for OMGPOP.

3. **Creativity cannot take a back seat to analytics**. The creative team needs a long leash. They have to trust their creative instincts or be

able to try new things even if the data (whether internal to the project or external to the marketplace) may point in another direction. In interviews, some Zynga managers have acknowledged the company may have gone too far with the data-driven approach, but by now it is so baked in to the company's culture it may be impossible to really give the creatives the freedom that they need.

Don Daglow, who started out as a video game programmer in the 1970s and rose through the ranks to become a games industry CEO, further believes Zynga alienated audiences with its intense focus on tweaking games to juice short-term revenue. "By ticking off their audience by pushing too hard on monetization they accelerated hundreds of millions in revenue . . . and threw away at least a couple of billion," he states.

Finding product-market fit for media

Finally, there's the issue of establishing product/market fit for new media. Of course it's possible to measure a media market, using revenue or audience size. For instance, in the United States, film brought in $29 billion in revenues in 2015. Local or niche markets can also be sized, such as the estimated $2.7 billion spent on broadcast TV advertising in California in 2017.

However, predicting future audience demand is extremely difficult. For one, there is a lot of fluidity within media market segments as audience preferences change. New genres can come out of nowhere. For instance, fiction for children and teens has cycled through numerous crazes over the years, ranging from "choose your own adventure" books in the 1980s to Harry Potter in the late 1990s and the recent fad for dystopian teen fiction. Conversely, what is hot one year may fade to irrelevance the next, as anyone who bothered to learn the "Gangnam Style" dance can attest. By comparison, the markets for light bulbs and insurance software are relatively predictable because customers' needs are so predictable.

Moreover, even if you create media that "fits" a particular market, there is no guarantee it will resonate. This is where intangibles can make an enormous difference, in ways that are not really a consideration in the markets that are targeted by a tech startup.

Take the market for energy-efficient light bulbs. Let's say a new firm designs a new LED bulb for home use. It glows like an incandescent bulb, but uses half as much power and lasts twice as long. Even better, the production costs are 1/10 that of incandescent bulbs and other competing technologies. It has found a sweet spot in the market, and the product is ready to take off. The new LED technology serves a clear customer need, and sales and profit should follow as long as the various production, distribution, and marketing pieces can be put into place. If intellectual property or exclusive distribution is involved, the technology may even establish a sustainable competitive advantage.

That's not the way media works, even if the market seems to be well-defined. First-person shooters (FPS), a popular video game genre, put players in the shoes of a soldier, cop, astronaut, vigilante, or zombie-slayer roaming a violent 3D world and shooting bad things. The market has existed since the 1990s and is well established, albeit splintered among various platforms (including the Xbox, PlayStation, and Windows PCs).

Let's say a game studio designs a new FPS title called *Replicant Genocide*. It fits the genre to a T. The backstory: Scientists working at a top-secret bioweapons lab in Area 51 lose control of an experimental virus engineered to create a synthetic super warrior. Authorities send in a team of special forces operatives to retake the lab and neutralize the crazed androids. The lab and desert areas are rendered using the latest 3D technologies. The game also uses standard interfaces to control player movement and actions, and incorporates dialogue recorded by professional actors. Other elements of the game are designed to appeal to the target demographic, teen boys and young men aged 14 to 22.

On the surface, *Replicant Genocide* may appear to have achieved product market fit. It's an FPS title, meets the basic standards of playability, and targets customers who regularly buy similar titles.

But here's the thing: Sales of *Replicant Genocide* may never take off. Gamers may be put off by the background music, the haircuts sported by the special forces operatives, the lack of health kits at the entrance to the bioweapons lab, or the unrealistic manner in which an infected replicant busts through a drop ceiling in level 3. The game may lack a sense of suspense, or the characters may not be particularly likable. Maybe the game comes out just as the target audience shifts to 2D arcade classics.

If *Replicant Genocide* were a light bulb, design or product flaws could be addressed through better engineering. But this is media, designed for entertainment and fun. Problems associated with intangible aspects of a game—or a song, website, book, or TV program—are not so easily engineered away.

Product development for light bulbs, gadgets, and business software focuses on features—what the product *does*. Media focuses on intangibles—how the experience *feels*.

If we accept that media products are fundamentally different than other types of products, then it follows that media creators need a different type of framework. It may borrow certain elements from Lean Manufacturing and Lean Startup, but there will be aspects of the framework that will be unique to our industry. In the next chapter, I will outline the principles that underlie Lean Media, using an example from the world of pop music.

Takeaways

- While Lean Manufacturing can be applied to industry, and Lean Startup is appropriate for many types of products and services, media is fundamentally different and requires a different type of framework.

- For media ventures, success may be correlated with sales, but creators also have a profound desire to make media that has unique creative, aesthetic, or artistic value.

- Audiences derive value from media in the visceral, intangible qualities of the experience, which may include excitement, pleasure, imagination, humor, understanding, or discovery.

- When the creative magic takes a backseat to media metrics, the end result tends to be milquetoast media that fails to impress audiences.

CHAPTER 4

Three Lean Media principles

Of all of the examples I have studied in the course of writing about Lean Media, the one that impresses me the most happens to be one of the oldest: the eponymous debut album by the British hard rock band Led Zeppelin. It is commonly referred to as "Led Zeppelin I" to differentiate it from the albums that followed. Besides having a fascinating backstory, the album serves as a great introduction to the three principles of Lean Media.

Led Zeppelin I is best known for the six-and-a-half-minute psychedelic masterpiece "Dazed and Confused." Two singles, "Good Times Bad Times" and "Communication Breakdown," generated a lot of radio airplay, too. The album also contained two blues tracks ("You Shook Me" and "I Can't Quit You Baby"), an acoustic ballad ("Babe I'm Gonna Leave You"), a short instrumental ("Black Mountain Side"), and a hippy sing-along ("Your Time Is Gonna Come").

Several of the tracks were originally composed by other artists, including "Dazed & Confused" (Jake Holmes), "Babe I'm Gonna Leave You" (Anne Bredon) and "You Shook Me" and "I Can't Quit You Baby" (Willie Dixon). Yet the songs were not mere covers. The members of Led Zeppelin applied their formidable talents and creativity to modify the songs with new riffs and new arrangements to make them their own.

If you are not familiar with the album, dig it out of your parents' record collection or hunt it down on a streaming music service. Not only is the album an example of great media, it distills three principles that define Lean Media:

1. Reduce waste

2. Understand audiences

3. Focus creativity

The following diagram shows the relationship between the three principles:

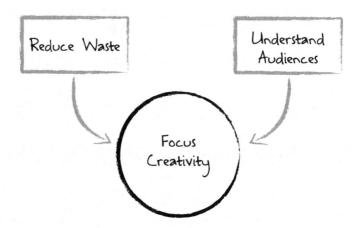

At a basic level, reducing waste while boosting understanding of audiences help the team focus its creativity.

Let's first take a look at what each of these three principles entail before moving on to Led Zeppelin.

Principle #1: Reduce waste

Media companies like to think big. When a new work is being developed, business and creative leaders may budget lots of resources—including people—in order to make the big vision a reality.

Unfortunately, more resources do not necessarily lead to better media. In fact, an excess of resources often leads to redundancy, friction, delays, and planning overhead.

Think about it. Doubling the size of a film crew doesn't double the quality of the movie. Nor does spending twice as much on instruments and other equipment make a band sound twice as good when they go out on tour. Sure, there might be some improvements in quality, or it may be possible to do things that would otherwise be difficult. But such benefits have to be evaluated against the added costs and the inevitable complications.

An example is The Who, one of Led Zeppelin's contemporaries. The Who's recording and touring success throughout the 1970s led them to make ever-increasing investments in amplifiers and other gear. At one point, bass player John Entwistle's sound rig was dubbed "Little Manhattan" for its towering size and multitude of blinking indicators. The gear enabled Entwistle to engage in a fruitless rivalry with guitarist Pete Townshend and drummer Keith Moon to be heard above each other, which drew the ire of singer Roger Daltrey.

In terms of quality, it is not the deafening live shows from the mid-1970s that The Who are remembered for. Rather, it is *Live at Leeds*, a recording from a medium-sized venue earlier in the band's career. The equipment at that time was far more modest, but it didn't matter—the band's energy, tightness, and talent made for a masterful performance and recording.

Unnecessary waste also manifests itself in the tendency for business leaders to grant stakeholders approvals and other forms of buy-in, often in the name of "promoting collaboration." Stakeholders may be internal (finance, sales, legal, or operations) or external (an investor, partner, or distributor) but the ultimate effect is the same: The creative team must spend extra time giving updates, asking for approval, and responding to various requests.

In a Lean Media project, reducing waste means removing unnecessary people, tools, processes, and bureaucracy. The purpose is to keep creative teams as lean as possible, speed up the development process, and budget just enough resources to create something great. By doing so, the creative core will be able to better concentrate on the media work itself, and not waste time and resources.

Principle #2: Understand audiences

In today's world, with near-universal reliance on digital production tools and distribution taking place on digital platforms, there is no shortage of quantitative data available to creative teams. Many ventures pay close attention to metrics regarding reach, sales, social sharing, and other audience interactions. But all of this takes place after the launch, not during the production when valuable insights might be gleaned from test audiences. During the production phase, the only feedback the team will hear is from other members of the team or business executives.

I can't tell you how many design committees I have been a part of over the years, for all kinds of media formats, from books to web video. Even though it has become far easier to gather usage data and poll audiences, the committees largely work the same way they did 20 or 30 years ago: Get the members in a conference room or gathered around a computer screen, and look at the different mockups the artists or graphic designer have put together. For almost all of these projects, the only feedback that ends up being used comes from team members or stakeholders, such as a sales executive or distribution partner. Even if the members tell themselves they are considering the interests of future audiences, it's actually their personal preferences and biases that determine the final design.

It's a huge leap of faith, topped with a large dollop of arrogance. And over the years I have seen many such design efforts fall flat when audiences finally get to see them post-launch.

Lean Media strives to break down these walls by learning from their audiences before the launch. As we will see in the example below, feedback from test audiences can help the creative team better understand who they are targeting, and make media that is more likely to resonate with real audiences.

Principle #3: Focus creativity

The creative team's job is to create great media. It's difficult to generalize what takes place at the center of this creative core. Every team and every project is different, but great media always involves talented people leveraging specialized tools and processes to produce works that touch their audiences in intangible and meaningful ways.

Focusing creativity means letting the members of the core creative team work together to achieve their creative vision with a minimum of interference and distraction (i.e., reducing waste). It also requires giving them access to information and other inputs that can help move the project forward (understanding audiences).

Rather than trying to explain the magic that takes place at the creative core, I will illustrate with a powerful example from the world of popular music.

Example: The making of Led Zeppelin I

Led Zeppelin I did not follow a typical path to chart-topping success for a late '60s rock band. There was little record company involvement in the album's production, and critics panned it. Yet *Led Zeppelin I* became phenomenally popular with audiences on both sides of the Atlantic, selling over 10 million copies. The band went on to become one of the top-grossing rock acts of the 1970s.

The band's backstory is also atypical. Led Zeppelin consisted of two experienced studio musicians (guitarist/founder Jimmy Page and bassist/keyboardist John Paul Jones) and two talented amateur musicians (singer Robert Plant and drummer John Bonham). Many rock bands of that era came up through the local club scene, playing in pubs and community halls. Some would eventually graduate to touring regional clubs and big cities if they were exceptionally talented and/or had a well-received song or album. This is how The Beatles got started. A few artists, such as The Jimi Hendrix Experience, had breakthroughs after playing major music festivals.

In contrast, the four members of Led Zeppelin were basically brought together by an unusual legal circumstance and Page's desire to quickly launch a new musical project. The band formed in August 1968 after Page's previous band, The Yardbirds, dissolved. However, The Yardbirds were still under contract to do a short Scandinavian tour. Page wanted to honor the contract and potentially get a new band off the ground. So he called around and cobbled together a group of stand-ins to complete the tour.

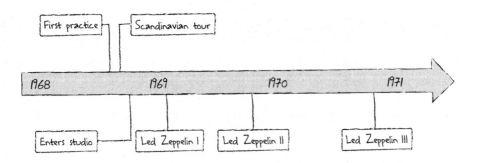

Page knew Jones from earlier recording sessions they had worked on. Plant and Bonham were relative unknowns who were members of Band of Joy, a local band from Birmingham, England. Page heard about Plant, and invited him to his home in London. There he determined they could get along musically and socially, which Page saw as a necessary ingredient for any new project. Plant mentioned he knew a good drummer, his friend and bandmate John Bonham. After Page saw Bonham play, he was brought on board.

The four members of the new band had little time to rehearse, but at the first practice session in London something clicked. There was incredible energy in the room, an indication that the project was destined to be more than a slapped-together cover band playing a one-off tour. It was in the rehearsal studio that the four men began to focus their creativity as they explored each other's musicianship, practiced cover songs, and started to write their own music.

After practicing for a few weeks, the band did the tour. They were billed as "The New Yardbirds." They played Yardbirds standards but branched out into blues covers and their own compositions. They also began to experiment with the songs and the order of the set list. For instance, "Dazed & Confused" was heavily modified as the band tried different sounds and textures, including Page's use of a violin bow to elicit ghostly notes from his instrument.

Importantly, the four musicians paid close attention to the reactions of the young people who came to their shows. The band used this feedback to shape future experiments. A new arrangement that resulted in bobbing heads, stomping feet, or wild applause might get higher placement at the next show. The tune that went over like a proverbial lead balloon might be demoted at later concerts, or removed from the setlist altogether. The concerts became an environment in which live feedback helped the four musicians iterate key arrangements—and validated the idea that they were more than a temporary effort. As Plant noted in a 1975 *Rolling Stone* interview, "We were learning what got us off most and what got people off most, and what we knew got more people back to the hotel after the gig."

Upon returning to England in September 1968, the renamed Led Zeppelin decided to enter the studio and cut an album. Again, the circumstances were unusual. A promising new band would typically have A&R executives and other record industry types hovering over them, appointing producers and studio musicians, deciding on track lists, and even pushing them to record certain types of songs based on the sounds or styles that were hot at the moment.

For Led Zeppelin, there was no record label involvement. The production team consisted of Page (who was the producer of the album), the three other members of the band, and a young studio engineer named Glyn Johns, who would later record or produce albums by Eric Clapton, Linda Ronstadt, and Nanci Griffith. The only other figure involved with the recording was the band's manager, a tough Londoner named Peter Grant. Page and Grant split the cost of the rented studio time.

Because they did not have much to spend and there was no record company interference, the work went quickly, taking just a few weeks from start to finish. The band recorded the songs live, with all four members playing simultaneously in the studio. There were a limited number of overdubs. Promising arrangements from the recently concluded Scandinavian tour figured prominently. Total recording time was between 30 and 36 hours, and cost less than $5,000.

With a full album's worth of songs in hand, Grant shopped around for a record label. It was an odd approach—usually a band wouldn't have studio recordings in hand—but the songs were good. The band was soon signed by New York-based Atlantic Records, and the album was officially launched in January 1969.

In less than 6 months, Led Zeppelin had gone from a group of stand-ins who barely knew each other to an up-and-coming creative force in the British rock scene. The band had a promising album under its belt and plans for an international tour and more recording. The release of *Led Zeppelin I* set the stage for global success.

Factors driving the band's success

While Led Zeppelin had no idea it was using Lean Media principles (*Led Zeppelin I* was recorded more than four decades before the framework was conceived), the album serves as an excellent example of Lean Media in action. It further serves as inspiration for modern creators who are interested in trying out Lean Media for themselves.

Returning to the three Lean Media principles listed above, the following factors contributed to the album's success:

Reducing waste

Single creative leader: Guitarist Jimmy Page brought the project together and controlled key aspects relating to compositions, arrangements, and recording. Other members of the team deferred to Page, speeding up decision-making and reducing potential friction.

Small creative team: The core creative team consisted of Page, Jones, Plant, and Bonham, with each person handling specific musical roles with limited overlap. Page had an additional creative role as producer of the album. As the recording engineer, Glyn Johns influenced the sound captured in the studio. Additional writers and musicians (many of them blues or folk musicians from previous decades) had songwriting roles, but they were not active participants in the Scandinavian tour or subsequent recording session. There was no artistic input or interference from Peter Grant, Led Zeppelin's business manager.

Small business team: There was only one business person associated with the group at this early stage—Grant. Because there was a single point of contact for business matters, Page and Grant could quickly make decisions. There were far fewer meetings than would have occurred had a record label been involved during the tour or recording.

Limited recording budget: The legal requirement to tour and the self-funded recording session encouraged Led Zeppelin to perfect the songs before they stepped into the studio. The band preferred recording their parts together, instead of instituting complex and time-consuming overdubs. The band did not hire studio musicians.

Understanding audiences

Validating audience interest: Jimmy Page ostensibly recruited Bonham, Jones, and Plant to satisfy an outstanding Yardbirds tour obligation. However, he was also interested in starting a new band. The live shows were a chance to test the idea of a new hard rock band playing new compositions along with arrangements of some old Yardbirds favorites. In addition, even though many audience members were expecting to see The Yardbirds, they clearly liked what they experienced, starting with the first "experimental concert," even though the lineup featured three unknown performers.

Feedback guides song development: The Scandinavian tour was an ideal opportunity for Led Zeppelin to try out new arrangements and new songs on live audiences. Applause, stomping feet, smiles, and other forms of audience feedback could help the band identify those songs and song elements that resonated with their target audience—young people interested in hard rock. Arrangements that did not resonate could be changed or dropped.

Feedback informs set list and recordings: An understanding of Led Zeppelin's live audience helped the band hone their live set and make decisions about the songs to be recorded. Two popular live songs, "You Shook Me" and "Dazed & Confused," were placed on the first side of the LP even though they were quite long and not particularly radio-friendly.

Focusing creativity

Prototyping songs while on tour: Led Zeppelin had neither the time nor the budget to gather at a creative retreat or write songs in a recording studio. Instead, the band wrote new compositions or reworked existing material while on tour. In other words, the tour effectively became a vehicle for prototyping the songs that would eventually appear on the album.

Quick iterative cycles: The rehearsal and touring cycle was compressed into a period lasting just 2 or 3 weeks. Iterative development of individual songs took place on a near-daily basis, based on what band members observed at the concerts. Once they entered the studio to record the album, iterations took place on an even tighter cycle, with internal feedback and insights from the studio engineer driving changes.

Minimal stakeholder interference: Record company executives were not involved with Led Zeppelin during the tour or recording sessions. Creative dynamics were therefore able to develop organically, without band members being pushed by label executives to support some supposed trend or market need. In addition, the team could quickly make creative decisions without having to consult with the label or wait for approvals. While the band did have a business manager and investor, he was more concerned with organizing tours and troubleshooting various business and logistical issues than meddling in creative issues.

The importance of the creative center

Creativity is the foundation of the Lean Media framework. This core is where team dynamics and creative ideas combine to make great media, whether it's a new song, website, book, or creative advertising campaign.

It is tempting to regard the two other Lean Media principles as potentially harmful to the creative foundation. For example, if reducing waste is a priority, then removing people or cutting the budget will surely make it more difficult for the creative team to perform. And if audience feedback drives creative decisions, the team is basically handing over the creative reins to the mob, right?

Not so! Reducing waste doesn't mean cutting indiscriminately. The key is to have a big enough team with the necessary resources to create great media without being bogged down by redundancy, meetings, approvals, distractions, and other non-essential, time-wasting elements.

In the autumn of 1968, Led Zeppelin was about as stripped-down as a band could be: It was just four musicians, a business manager, a small road crew, and a recording engineer. Key people were in place and had their assigned roles. The four members could work on music without a lot of business or process overhead. They used the tour to practice and perfect the songs, and had just enough money and time to record a full-length album.

As for audience feedback, it should be seen as a way to understand audiences and inform decision-making, rather than an automatic creative override. Indeed, creators should feel empowered to trust their own instincts over audience preferences, and ignore certain feedback if it clashes with the team's sensibilities.

For instance, the lead track on *Led Zeppelin I* was not the song that received the most enthusiastic feedback on tour. Instead, it was "Good Times Bad Times," a song the band rarely played live. Even though Page didn't have much feedback to go on, the band knew the song was catchy. It was also relatively short, which increased the chance of radio airplay. It was therefore placed first on the album, ahead of the other songs the band recorded in the studio.

Lean Media for small projects

Lean Media is not only for large, complicated projects such as an album, website, or TV drama. It's possible to use it for a five-minute-long web video, a short story, or magazine feature. Lean Media methods can also be applied to a small element of a larger project, such as an individual song, a scene in a movie, the cover of a book, or even the headline for a news article.

One advantage of using Lean Media for small projects is the team almost always consists of just a handful of people and is therefore much easier to coordinate. This embodies the principle of reducing waste. In terms of understanding audiences, feedback is usually easier to gather because creators are not asking for audiences to spend as much time evaluating a prototype. As an author, it's easier for me to ask people to read a single chapter rather than the entire manuscript. In fact, this is exactly what I did for this book, with early chapters appearing on the leanmedia.org blog for potential readers to evaluate!

Here's another example of a small Lean Media project. At most newspapers and online news websites, it takes just a few minutes for a reporter and editor to toss around ideas for a catchy headline. Getting feedback from audiences will take a few hours at most. Some online news sites have systems that make it easy to A/B test different versions of the headline on real audiences and then automatically go with the version that has the highest click-through rate. Other publications might use social media or a dedicated reader panel to help with feedback.

Takeaways

The three principles of Lean Media—reducing waste, understanding audiences, and focusing creativity—serve as the foundation of the Lean Media framework. Practically speaking, this means media ventures should:

- Keep creative/production teams as lean as possible.
- Budget just enough resources to create something great.
- Scale back meetings, approvals, bureaucracy, and other unnecessary processes.
- Let test audiences learn about the product or experience actual prototypes early and often.
- Use feedback to understand audiences and gain insights into the media being produced.
- Iterate quickly.

5

The Lean Media flowchart

The three principles of reducing waste, understanding audiences, and focusing creativity define the Lean Media framework. Another aspect of Lean Media involves mapping feedback cycles against the production workflow. The Lean Media flowchart described below provides a visual reference for creators to evaluate how their own unique processes can be augmented by Lean Media.

Let's first revisit the chubby flowchart from Chapter 2. As mentioned, this was the dominant model for making and releasing media throughout much of the 20th century, and is still widespread in book publishing, popular music, big-budget films, console gaming, and other fields. Here's how it works:

- Media is conceived by creators, management, owners, or investors.

- Creators retreat to their studios, rehearsal rooms, and desks where they develop and perfect the media in secret.

- Marketers designate a date for the chubby launch, and coordinate advertising and press coverage of the finished product.

- Audiences may get brief glimpses of the media via the marketing campaign, but are otherwise not exposed to the final product until after the launch.

- The media work is regarded as "fixed" upon launch, and will probably not be revised unless it is a serial media (such as a TV show) or a new digital format (such as a website or game).

Here's what the chubby flowchart looks like:

Chubby media is ubiquitous. Most readers of this book have undoubtedly participated in the creation or marketing of works that are made in secret and launched with a bang. One of my first part-time media jobs in college was a licensed projectionist for the single-screen Janus Theater in Harvard Square in Cambridge, Massachusetts. At the beginning of each week, I had to splice short previews (also known as trailers) of upcoming releases onto the front of *Babette's Feast, Who Framed Roger Rabbit,* and other films. The previews included brief clips of already-completed films that had yet to be released to the public. Then, as now, previews were a crucial part of blockbuster marketing. The goal: to build hype and to have a strong box office on the first weekend that carries the momentum for weeks or even months.

When the chubby model works, it can lead to a splash that results in lots of buzz and ticket sales. The problem for creators and the media ventures they work for is this model does not always work. In fact, the chubby model has a terrible track record. On any given holiday weekend there will be a score of new movie releases, but only a handful will experience blockbuster success. Others will do moderately well and manage to make a modest profit, or at least recoup the production and marketing costs. The remainder will fail, sometimes spectacularly so.

The model persists in other areas of the media industry. For instance, a big New York publishing house might collaborate with an author over a period of many years to prepare a novel for publication. A few months before the official launch, readers will begin to see advertisements for the upcoming release, and a select few will get review copies so Amazon, Goodreads, and other online sites will have reader reviews when the book formally launches. Professional reviews will appear in *The New York Review of Books, Foreword Reviews, Library Journal,* and other publications. The author will start a publicity tour. The goal is to build interest and hype the title so sales take off and remain strong for many months or years.

Thousands of titles follow this launch model every year, yet there are very few breakout hits. Well over 90% of books signed to publishing houses fail, meaning they do not earn back the advances paid out to authors. Meanwhile, the number of Americans who read books is slowly declining in the face of competition from digital devices, which provide easy access to music, news, games, and video content. The results of the 2016 Nielsen survey below show the percentage of American adults who said they had recently purchased any kind of book.

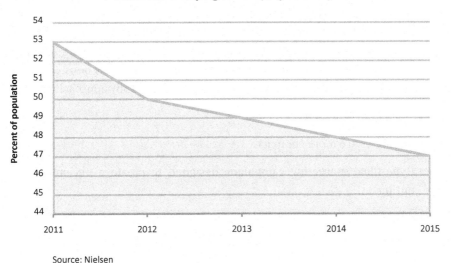

Americans buying books (any format)

Source: Nielsen

So why do movie studios, book publishers, and other media companies continue to use an incredibly wasteful and risky model?

Part of the reason relates to the potential for a massive success with lots of interest, sales, and accolades. There will likely be a huge payout to the key creative and business players, not to mention a reputation boost that can lead to new opportunities and a lifelong claim to a big win.

There are other factors that contribute to the continued reliance on the chubby model. Critically, marketers, ad agencies, and publicists are incentivized to favor a big, hype-filled launch—the intense work leads to higher salaries and fees.

Moreover, for many in the industry—whether on the creative side, business, or marketing side—it is the only approach they know. It's what they learn in school, it's how media has always been launched at their own organizations, it's how their competitors launch new media, and it seems to work from time to time. Why bother doing it any other way?

A flowchart for media productions

Lean Media presents an alternate way of developing and launching media. Not only is it different from the chubby approach, but it also reduces costs and risk and is more likely to lead to media that audiences love. Lean Media does not guarantee a profit, but it makes it far easier for creators to leverage existing business models to work in their favor. That might mean more paid downloads, higher-priced concert tickets or bigger concert venues, extending the theater run, better click-through rates, bigger advances, higher royalty rates, more effective campaigns, or more favorable distribution deals.

Let's go back to the Lean Media principles covered in the previous chapter. Creativity lies at the center of the framework. On one side, it is boosted by the lean principle of reducing waste. Differences with the chubby approach include:

- Teams can be smaller.

- Timelines are more compact.

- Hype-filled marketing campaigns designed to create a big splash are optional.

In other words, Lean Media practitioners can scale back time-consuming planning, coordination tasks, and approvals, not to mention expensive advertising.

Creativity is further boosted by an understanding of the audience. Practically speaking, this means the magic that takes place within the creative core is augmented by feedback from audiences. This feedback can be gathered as early as the moment of ideation, when the initial creative spark occurs or when the proposal is put forward. Feedback continues through the iterative cycles of prototyping and improving the media, allowing the core team to better understand audiences and to gain insights into the media they are working on. While some teams may opt for a hard, fixed launch, there is no requirement to do so. Lean Media encourages a flexible launch that allows for further rounds of feedback and iteration.

Importantly, the risk associated with not knowing what audiences will think is reduced, because creators will be getting feedback from test audiences starting at a much earlier stage. Ideally, by the time the flex launch rolls around, the creative team (and the marketing group, if there is one) will know their creation has a good chance of resonating with audiences, because test audiences have already told them they love it! If it doesn't resonate, it's still possible to keep iterating after the launch.

While this cycle has parallels with the human-centered design framework espoused by design firms such as IDEO as well as the d.school at Stanford University, there is a key difference: With the Lean Media framework, the creative vision and idea always starts with the team. Followers of the human-centered design framework strive to achieve an understanding of users through observation before ideation takes place.

Conceptually, the Lean Media flowchart looks like this:

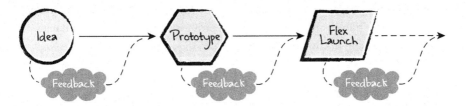

A few notes about the terminology:

- The **idea** can be a simple proposal, description, outline, sketch, or wire-frame that can be discussed by the core team and perhaps a small number of potential audience members.

- I have opted to use "**prototype**" to describe early versions of new media prior to the launch. Not only is it easy to understand, but it also conveys the iterative nature of Lean Media projects. The first prototype will be rough, but over many iterations it will reach a fairly polished state. Polished prototypes make it easier to gather useful feedback from test audiences, but it is still possible to leverage early prototypes, as we will see below.

- Lean Media launches are **flexible**—they can be hard, soft, or staggered. Hard launches are more or less fixed; the team has no intention to iterate further and will move onto new projects afterwards. In contrast, a soft launch involves releasing a product to a small group of audience members in order to gauge interest, tweak features, and adjust marketing before the formal rollout. Staggered launches usually involve serial or multiformat media in which later versions draw upon the failures and successes of earlier releases. In a Lean Media context, the flex launch version is highly polished, in a final or near-final state, and is available to the public. It can be quietly launched to a subset of the marketplace, such as a limited geographic area or a single distribution channel, or it can be launched in connection with a major marketing campaign across the entire country.

- **Feedback** can be qualitative (i.e., based on audience comments or observations of their behavior) or quantitative (i.e., based on metrics or other forms of numerical data). In addition, while feedback doesn't have to be gathered for each stage, the earlier it is available, the more useful it will be. Creators will be able to leverage the input to better understand their audiences and make informed decisions about how to improve the media.

Here's an example. Not long ago, I used the Lean Media framework to prepare a medium-sized magazine article about Amazon's self-serve advertising platform, which book publishers can use to promote new titles or their backlists.

Feedback began at the ideation phase. During a chat with several independent publishers, I mentioned that I had tried the Amazon self-serve advertising platform for my own books, and had experienced a positive return on the investment. They were curious about my experience and urged me to write an article for *IBPA Independent*, the magazine of the Independent Book Publishers Association (of which I am a member). The feedback at this stage validated the interest in the topic and support for an article that could be shared more widely in the publisher community.

After my pitch was accepted by the magazine's editor, it took me about three hours to write a first draft (the prototype stage in the flowchart). I sent the draft article back to an expanded group of publishers who provided more qualitative feedback. While several test readers said the article was informative and provided useful tips, one reader wanted to know more details about choosing keywords and setting bid levels for an Amazon ad campaign. Another suggested letting readers know how long it takes to evaluate a new ad campaign. I incorporated some of their suggestions for the next draft, which I sent to the editor. However, I also disregarded a few comments from my test readers—as the creator of the article, I felt it wasn't necessary to answer every question or explore all of the angles they suggested.

The print format and the fact I volunteered to write it favored a hard launch. I had no intention to modify it or follow up after it was published. However, there were other possibilities within a Lean Media flex launch. Once the article appeared online, myself and the magazine staff could have used both quantitative feedback (such as website views and social shares) as well as qualitative feedback (online comments from readers) to further improve the article—or make plans for a follow-up.

As this example demonstrates, the feedback cycles in the Lean Media flowchart can make a powerful difference. My test audience had specific questions and observations that not only led to a topic that was more likely to resonate, but also helped improve the draft before it reached the editor.

This is much different than the process I would have used ten years earlier. Even if I had managed to identify a suitable topic, I would not have received any constructive feedback from test audiences before it was published. The final version of the article would have therefore been far less likely to connect with real audiences once it was released.

Modes Vu's photography books

N.E.O. Bernhardsson, a Hong Kong-based publisher of art photography books, reached out to me after reading about Lean Media online. His venture, called Modes Vu, leverages a low-cost system of digital and print prototypes to produce *MODES*, a series of art books that feature the work of young photographers, many of them from China.

Bernhardsson previously worked on an independent, pocket-sized art/photography/fashion publication. The magazine used traditional publishing processes, which had several downsides. "Each issue was over 200 pages and took a year to complete," he recalls. "This was taxing for everyone involved because it felt like a long slog with no feedback until a year later."

Bernhardsson also found the chubby approach was problematic at a commercial magazine he worked on, as well. For example, when conflicts arose, the team would sometimes have to scrap an entire issue, and start re-planning it from scratch. It was wasteful and frustrating.

Following these experiences, Bernhardsson and his collaborators contemplated an alternative mode of publishing that would leverage inexpensive digital printing technologies and an iterative development process.

The Modes Vu model has a slight twist: At the ideation stage, Modes Vu is not involved. Rather, the photographers—most of them outsiders or relative unknowns in the world of art photography—use smartphones to independently publish their work on social networking websites. The Modes Vu team approaches promising photographers to make a prototype printed book of their photographs.

"We come in here after seeing their photographs on Tumblr or Instagram, and make an edit of 48 images out of their likely hundreds of images," Bernhardsson states. "In some cases, the photographer has a clear concept/idea, but more often they are shooting intuitively and capturing images of a similar type and sensibility."

A single photographer may have published hundreds of images online, but working with the Modes Vu editorial team, 48 are selected for the first print prototype, the Workbook. The books are tiny, just 4.5 inches by 6 inches, not much bigger than a postcard. A second prototype stage known as "Greens" uses a slightly larger 6-by 9-inch format, higher-quality paper, two-page spreads, and a green cover (visit leanmedia.org to see samples).

"We didn't want to have a typical artist book design with a clean white background, but instead chose a green color that would stand out more in shops and at book fairs," Bernhardsson explains. "A second idea is that some of the books grow and shoot off green sprouts, which become the second edition, a Green." The Chinese name for the Greens is 小草, literally "little grass."

After a Workbook is released, audience feedback as well as the judgment of the editorial team will determine whether the work will progress to a Green. If it is given the go-ahead, feedback and discussions determine which photographs will be published in the Green, but the team also evaluates new photographs. Feedback includes raw sales numbers as well as likes, page views, and reblogs of individual pages that are posted online.

As the artists are not well-known, sales of the Workbooks and Greens are limited, which means high-quality offset printing is out of the question. Instead, Modes Vu uses an inexpensive digital printing technology called print on demand (POD), which can produce a single copy at a low cost—readers typically pay $15 for a Workbook and $20 for one of the Greens. The layouts of the books are standard, which also keeps costs down.

The Green is also evaluated by the team and posted online to gather feedback. Not all Greens will make it to the final stage, but those projects that are accepted will be turned into a high-quality photo book 9 inches wide by 12 inches tall, between 80 and 100 pages long, and featuring the work of a single photographer. *MODES No. 1: JAM* is scheduled to be released in 2017 at a retail price of $30.

Modes Vu is an example of Lean Media in action. The principles of reducing waste, understanding audiences, and concentrating the creative talents of the team lie at the core of the venture. Having a standard, explicit process is key to managing the workflow; not only does it keep costs down but it also helps manage expectations—photographers, editors, designers, and other team members know what to expect. Throughout the production, feedback drives iterative cycles and helps the team make decisions about which books should be greenlit to the next stage:

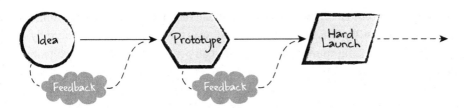

The Lean Media flowchart shows feedback taking place throughout the production, and ending with the launch. Bernhardsson says the release of the MODES is treated as a hard launch with no plans to iterate. However, I can't help but think that post-launch feedback from the early MODES is likely to inform the future development of the series. This is what happened with *The Simpsons*, our next Lean Media example.

A lean history of *The Simpsons*

The Simpsons is a massively popular cartoon program, beloved by hundreds of millions of people across the world. As mentioned in Chapter 1, I used to think the early success of *The Simpsons* had a lot to do with vision (a great program backed by a risk-taking network) and competitive factors (no one else was doing a prime-time cartoon series). But when I applied the lens of Lean Media, a new narrative emerged.

The Simpsons was the brainchild of Matt Groening. Hollywood legend has it that the idea was nothing more than a sketch on a napkin he presented to the upstart Fox Broadcasting Company. Fox liked the concept of a dysfunctional yellow-skinned family, but executives were not ready to invest in a full-fledged animated sitcom. Instead, they greenlit a series of animated shorts that could be played during another comedy program that the network was trying to get off the ground.

Groening showed early sketches to peers and collaborators, but it is not clear if he sought feedback on the idea from test audiences. In his view, it may not have been necessary: Some of Groening's earlier work (including the off-beat print cartoon *Life in Hell*) were already established underground hits. He and his backers at Fox may have assumed that audiences would be similarly amused by a weird, animated family.

The Simpsons debuted in 1987 as 90-second "bumper" that appeared before commercial breaks on *The Tracey Ullman Show*, Fox's new sketch comedy program. Because *Simpsons* segments were so short and piggybacked onto another program, they were relatively inexpensive to produce. It was a good thing, too—Fox did not have the same financial resources as the three dominant broadcasters (ABC, CBS, and NBC). "Cheap" was the only thing that would fly.

The Simpsons bumpers can be regarded as prototypes. The creative team's budget was limited, so the clips were short, hurriedly recorded, and roughly animated. Instead of full storylines with a variety of settings, the bumpers usually showed the family in a static shot (such as sitting on a couch), delivering one-off jokes and slapstick gags.

Fox gathered quantitative feedback about The Tracey Ullman Show. The data included television ratings that showed the number of viewers in each metropolitan market as well as the share of the total audience watching television at the time of the broadcast. The metrics for The Tracey Ullman Show were not encouraging, but it was not clear how people reacted to The Simpsons because the ratings did not break out data for individual sketches or segments within the show.

Qualitative feedback told a different story. There was a strong positive buzz about The Simpsons. Audiences regarded the short clips as quirky and entertaining. I was in college at the time, and remember that my friends and I considered The Simpsons to be the best part of The Tracey Ullman Show.

After the program had been running for many months, The Simpsons team was able to gather audience feedback from another source. As a sketch comedy show filmed in front of a live studio audience, Tracey Ullman and the rest of the cast had to take frequent breaks to change costumes and rearrange the set. To keep the studio audience entertained, the team spliced dozens of 90-second Simpsons bumpers into 20-minute reels and showed them during these breaks. It was a hit! The resulting laughter validated the idea that The Simpsons could be developed into a full-length program.

Fox decided to give it a shot. In December 1989, The Simpsons launched as a half-hour prime time sitcom under the direction of James L. Brooks (who also produced The Tracey Ullman Show and co-created the sitcom Taxi) and showrunner Sam Simon (another Taxi and Ullman Show colleague, as well as a writer on the sitcom Cheers).

There was a lot of uncertainty around the program. Fox was not fully convinced a non-traditional program—a cartoon aimed at adults—could do well in a prime-time slot. The Simpsons also arrived in the middle of the television season, with the writing and animation teams still trying to figure out how to make it work as a half-hour sitcom.

But the uncertainty quickly faded. Audience feedback indicated the team had a hit on its hands. The Simpsons had wide appeal across different demographic groups, with kids and adults tuning into the show. By the spring of 1990, it was one of the top ten prime time shows in terms of ratings. There was also massive demand for Simpsons merchandise, from toys to T-shirts. *The Simpsons* team was on the right track.

The Simpsons was also a case in which there was no need for a nuclear-powered launch. There was a marketing push in all metropolitan markets with Fox affiliates, but *The Simpsons* already had a fanbase thanks to two years of bumpers on *The Tracey Ullman Show*. Word-of-mouth recommendations and widespread (and often unsolicited) press coverage ensured that nearly everyone in the United States knew about *The Simpsons* by the end of the first season.

If *The Simpsons* were modeled on a modified Lean Media flowchart, it would look like this:

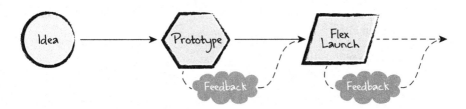

In Lean Media terms, the December 1989 flex launch of the prime-time cartoon program was typical for weekly television programs and other serial media. As the season progressed, the team was willing to make improvements based on what they were learning about their audience as well as their own creative instincts. Some early episodes were made in response to public controversies about the show, including one that featured Marge Simpson starting an activist group to protest violence on television and another that lampooned the presidency of George H. W. Bush (which the team produced after the president criticized *The Simpsons* for promoting poor behavior).

Early success allowed the team to scale its efforts. Brooks and Simon could go out and hire great writers, animators, and voice talent. Success also allowed the team to demand—and receive—creative autonomy from the network. While other shows had to put up with various creative demands from the network to control costs or boost ratings among certain demographic segments, Fox executives did not interfere with *The Simpsons*. The team could pretty much do what it wanted, and its members pushed the envelope. Examples include the introduction of a gay character (Smithers) as well as an annual Halloween special that involved members of the family being killed off by monsters, aliens, and psychopaths. From time to time writers would take aim at Fox executives or other Fox programming, as well.

By the third or fourth season, *The Simpsons* team hit its stride with a formula that audiences adored. The team established *The Simpsons* as one of the best programs on network television. More than 25 years later, it is still going strong, and has spawned an empire of merchandise, films, songs, and even a theme park ride at Universal Studios.

Touchpoints for feedback

Applying the Lean Media framework to the development of *The Simpsons* reveals the importance of both qualitative and quantitative feedback. For other media productions, qualitative feedback may be more accessible, particularly during the early prototyping stages. Feedback may cover:

- Design elements

- Aesthetic considerations

- How the media makes audiences feel (intangibles)

- Pricing

We will take a closer look at test audiences and methods for gathering feedback later in the book. Before we close out the chapter, it's worth quickly running through potential touchpoints for gathering feedback.

Ideally, audiences will share feedback with the team at the earliest stages of development, starting with the idea itself. It is unlikely a prototype will be ready the day your brilliant plan is hatched, but for certain formats it will be possible to talk with audiences about the concept, or show a simple outline or wireframe. Use those comments to understand your audience and to inform development of first prototypes.

Let's say you have an idea for FishBuddies, a website covering the latest developments in the world of home aquariums and fishponds. To determine if the idea is viable, you could create a simple website landing page with some marketing copy and design mockups. Social media and cheap online advertising could drive people to the landing page, where you could gather qualitative and quantitative feedback using a simple online form. For instance, you could have respondents rate the idea on a scale of 1 to 10, or ask them about what types of content they would like to see on the site (e.g., articles, photo galleries, community features, or "how-to" videos). The results could help inform the creative team working on the design and editorial content.

Landing page with a survey form to gather feedback from potential audience members.

Once a working prototype is available, don't keep it under wraps—let your test audiences try it out! Take note of which pages or features they use most often, and ask them to comment on the experience. Use the feedback from the test sessions to shape progressive iterations of the prototype.

After a few months, it will be time to for the flex launch. The FishBuddies site will be highly polished and ready for the public. The launch can be limited to a geographic area or a single distribution channel, or it can be released nationally with a splashy marketing campaign (no pun intended). Assuming test audiences have become progressively more enthusiastic about the prototypes, you and the rest of the creative team should have a good sense of how real audiences will react when they see the site.

However, the flexible launch also leaves the door open to further changes in design, content, and other elements. Depending on how audiences react to the flex launch, FishBuddies may only need some minor tweaks—or it could require a major overhaul. If it really takes off, it can be expanded to a mobile app or a print magazine if the team determines the demand is sufficient.

Takeaways

- Lean Media incorporates feedback cycles into the idea, prototype, and flex launch stages. This differs from the chubby approach, which does not have audience feedback mechanisms built into the production stages.

- An idea can be a concept ("a romantic comedy set in Singapore"), an outline, a simple sketch, or a basic wireframe.

- Prototypes can range from a very basic demo, rough draft, or raw footage to a fairly polished version.

- The flex launch version is highly polished and ready for public consumption. Creators may want to take a soft launch approach by limiting its distribution as they evaluate audience reaction and make improvements.

6

Building a Lean Media team

The creative team is the heart of any media development project. At the very least, the creative team will produce the work. In many cases, the team is also responsible for developing and implementing the creative vision.

For some teams, there may also be business responsibilities that involve sales, marketing, and operations. However, professional media companies usually have a separate business group that handles such issues.

There is tremendous variation in the size and makeup of creative teams, and whether they follow lean principles or work according to a more traditional model. Some will be so small they can hardly be considered a team at all, consisting of just a single creative lead and perhaps a few affiliates to cover gaps in production. The solo musician, author, or an independent game developer are examples.

At the other end of the spectrum are the gigantic teams which are responsible for producing a big-budget movie, television show, news website, or console video game. There might be hundreds of people involved, all with specific roles and responsibilities, and managed under a vertical organizational structure with strict lines of command.

Oftentimes, the creative vision will be dictated by a business leader ("let's do a sequel!") or perhaps from an outsider such as a writer who submits a promising screenplay. The business executive or the independent writer may have no direct involvement in the creation of the final work; it's up to the director or production lead to take the idea and run with it, leveraging the abilities and creative instincts of the team. However, the business leader may also be the creative leader (or a key member of the creative team) and will have deep input in the development of new media.

Creative teams can be fluid, with members or affiliates switching in and out of the team as the project progresses or different skill sets are tapped. Consider a publisher who wants to launch a new regional tourism magazine. She may come up with the vision, but it will be quickly handed off to a small creative team that includes the art director and editor-in-chief (EIC). This small group will work on the initial mockups and editorial plan. As decisions are made concerning the appearance and voice of the new publication, the art director and EIC will step back. Junior staff will take on the myriad implementation tasks required, from finessing the designs of individual pages to setting up a content management system and hiring copy editors.

By the time the launch occurs, the EIC and lead designer will have little day-to-day interaction with the expanded creative team. Their jobs will mainly be associated with preserving the vision established by the publisher (who now handles business matters, including circulation, sales, and operations), putting out fires, and managing the team. The day-to-day tasks associated with publishing articles, commissioning photographs, and laying out the next issue will fall on the managing editor, the senior designer, and the reporters, photo editors, copy editors, and other staff.

Who leads a Lean Media team?

Led Zeppelin circa 1968 had a clear creative leader—Jimmy Page. In addition to developing the vision of a hard-rock band with blues and psychedelic roots, Page recruited the musicians, decided on the initial tour set list, and served as the producer of the album.

Another well-known Lean Media project, Minecraft, also had a single creative leader. Markus "Notch" Persson had a vision for a virtual world based on building things, from simple houses to elaborate dungeons. Minecraft eventually became one of the most popular video game franchises ever devised, and was sold to Microsoft for $2.5 billion in 2014.

As with many media ventures, while the Minecraft team was still small, the creative leader was also the business leader. Notch made all of the business decisions, ranging from setting prices to choosing which platforms to expand to. Erik Bernhardsson, the editor of the Modes Vu photography books described in Chapter 5, also handles the business side of the venture.

At other times, the business is run by a completely different team. Most newspapers, magazines, and websites with editorial content employ separate groups to handle subscriptions, advertising, events, and other revenue-generating activities. This is how *Huffington Post, National Geographic,* and other publications operate.

Not all Lean Media projects have a clear creative lead. In certain situations, the role may be shared by different people as the project progresses or the original leader steps aside. In others, the members of the creative team may reach an agreement (tacit or otherwise) that results in leadership being shared.

Many people assume the creative leader in the early days of *The Simpsons* was Matt Groening. The cartoonist came up with the vision of the dysfunctional animated family, and today is listed as the creator in the show credits. He even received his own star on the Hollywood Walk of Fame.

However, prior to *The Simpsons*, Groening had never done any animation work and had no experience writing sitcoms. The hard work associated with bringing *The Simpsons* to the small screen fell upon two other people: Producer James L. Brooks, who came up with the idea of creating a prime time animated sitcom and oversaw the development of *The Simpsons* starting in 1987; and the late Sam Simon, the showrunner and executive producer who led the writing team for the show's first four seasons. Without Brooks, *The Simpsons* would never have existed. Without Simon, it probably would not have enjoyed the early success that it did.

As one might expect, shared leadership comes with special challenges. There are often big egos or management pressure, and the atmosphere can become charged. Paradoxically, rivalries In the core team can feed a creative tension that results in amazing work. On *The Simpsons*, Groening and Simon reportedly could not stand each other and rarely spoke. Groening and Brooks also had a tense relationship that on occasion blew up in public. Nevertheless, the three men and the rest of the team were able to produce brilliant work that entertained millions and redefined a genre.

In situations in which there is a clashing creative leadership, it helps if the rivals have clearly defined areas of responsibility and processes for resolving conflicts—and are able to keep pushing forward even if there is a breakdown in communications.

How small should the team be?

As noted earlier, the Lean Media principle of reducing waste means that the creative team should have just enough people and resources to create great media.

The idea of having "just enough" may seem strange to media organizations programmed to think big, and are used to approving large budgets for new projects and assigning lots of people to get the job done. Good intentions are often at work—the company wants to ensure the project will be completed on time, the quality is top-notch, and all relevant stakeholders are collaborating with the core team. In some cases, business leaders stuff creative teams with too many talented people, in the belief that putting all of the best people on the project will yield superior results.

Adding more people to a media project does not lead to linear improvements in speed, quality, or impact. Quite often it leads to delays, internal friction, and unnecessary work—the antithesis of reducing waste. It takes more effort to get 15 people in the same room for a kickoff meeting, compared to a small group of just 5 or 6 people. With a lot of heavy hitters in the room, egos may clash. And consider what happens when the creative team is forced to seek approvals from internal stakeholders in sales, legal, distribution, and finance, as well as external stakeholders working for partner companies. Extra time has to be inserted into the production schedule to accommodate them. Some stakeholders may fail to respond in time, causing further delays.

There is also a risk of stakeholders inserting additional requirements into the project that were not envisioned by the creative team. Some will be minor but time-consuming, while others can throw a wrench into the works, causing major delays, additional costs, and headaches. Here are some examples:

- The band planned an album with 10 songs, but now the music label wants five more tunes including a dance mix and a collaboration with another artist on the same label. This will require two more weeks in the studio, not to mention a special round of negotiations with the guest artist to discuss various creative and business considerations. The launch will be delayed by many months.

- The team of writers and video producers had an idea for a web video series, but executives who control the purse strings demand that the format be changed into something that can be distributed on cable television. The team will have to rewrite the first ten episodes to fit the half-hour format preferred by cable networks, and use more expensive cameras, audio, and lighting rigs to meet cable TV's higher production standards.

- The business news website was supposed to cover a single vertical—the healthcare industry—but the sales team says the focus will need to be expanded to pharmaceuticals. This will put off the launch by two months as the team scrambles to hire more reporters and editors, and the web developers and designers rework the site's navigation and other features.

I have witnessed these types of scenarios play out. In the early 1990s, I worked for The KLF, one of Britain's top pop recording acts. Whenever the duo attempted to bring on guest singers or rappers, it was never straightforward. No matter how obscure or famous the guest artist was, there were invariably delays, negotiations, and sniping. Business managers and record label representatives often inserted themselves into the fray, adding more complexity and frustration.

Once, a little-known guest rapper with a huge ego insisted that he had to be driven to and from the recording studio in a limousine. Another time an agreement to have country singer Tammy Wynette perform on a KLF remix was almost scuttled after various business stakeholders butted heads. Then there was the guest singer who came back many months after the song she sang on was released, insisting on thousands of pounds in additional payments because the song had become a huge hit. Contractually, this singer didn't have a leg to stand on. Nevertheless, she got her money—The KLF's label manager later told me it just wasn't worth the time or effort to fight it out in court.

For people who are tasked with putting together a Lean Media team—typically an experienced creative leader or the CEO of a media company—a different approach is required. One of the first orders of business: Avoid overloading the team. Ask hard questions concerning redundancy and overlap. For instance:

- How many studio engineers and technicians are needed to get the album done?

- How many scriptwriters are required for a new sitcom pilot?

- For a website redesign, will having two graphic designers really speed things up?

- How many outside collaborators are required to complete a production?

Slimming down a team can be difficult, especially in established media organizations. For a big Hollywood studio, London publishing house, or New York marketing agency, people think big. It's assumed a new project will have a correspondingly large team. Operating in slim mode will be seen as going against cultural norms.

Another situation that sometimes occurs involves a hot new project everyone wants to be involved in. For the creative lead, it will be necessary to steel his or her jaw and choose just enough people to make great media. For those who don't get a chance to take part, there will be hurt feelings, but in the long run it gives the project a better chance of succeeding.

In addition, creatives need to approach meetings in a different way. They should be scheduled only on an as-needed basis. Further, the agenda should concentrate on those issues that need to be discussed, and nothing more. An effective technique is to start with a "bottom line up front" (BLUF) declaration at the beginning of the meeting, which succinctly bullets out the goal(s) and minimizes discussion of tangential issues.

Status updates should be just that—a summary of how the project is proceeding. Creatives should avoid asking for feedback on the actual media being developed unless someone's opinion truly needs to be taken into consideration.

When nonessential stakeholders get in the way

Another area of concern for Lean Media practitioners relates to approvals. Many media businesses insist on non-creative people getting involved in the decision-making process. This may include senior executives, salespeople, in-house counsel, clients, investors, and employees of partner companies.

This type of involvement can turn into a draining, distracting morass. In most cases, their input does little to improve the media. Bede McCarthy, director of product for the *Financial Times* website, states that "any kind of sign-off process slows things down and doesn't help customers." The *Financial Times'* customers—paying subscribers to the website—simply want access to great articles, information, and site features. The audience is not well-served by delays that prevent the team from improving the site.

There are several reasons why suits get involved in the creative side of the business. Many companies require such approvals for unique reasons relating to internal politics, company culture, and precedent. Others attempt to follow modern management practice, which emphasizes collaboration and buy-in from separate groups in order to align stakeholder interests. Regardless of the reason, sign-offs are not optional—they *must* take place or the project won't be able to move forward.

Let's not mince words. Lean Media is a different approach to creating media. Practitioners do not follow standard management practice. Emphasis is placed on eliminating waste, focusing creativity, and understanding audiences. Anything that does not align with these principles must be reconsidered.

When it comes to non-creative stakeholders, this may entail minimizing their roles, or even removing them altogether. As you can imagine, this will not go over well in some quarters. People like feeling involved in the creative process and exerting control, even if it is little more than a perfunctory approval.

In a Lean Media environment, involving non-creative stakeholders means the creative team has to deal with time-wasting meetings, whimsical requests, and other delays that take them away from making great media. In some cases, a high-level business executive or investor can insist on changes that utterly compromise the work.

At the end of the day, the only stakeholders whose opinion truly matters are audience members. The creative musings of a sales V.P. or lead investor are unlikely to yield audience insights or help the core team focus its creativity, and can therefore be regarded as waste.

That said, there are legitimate non-creative inputs which require attention. The in-house legal counsel of a large media company may have to sign off on any copyright-related matters for a new video series. A big investor in a Hollywood film may insist on getting involved in script revisions and on-set decisions as conditions of providing funding. An advertising agency will need to present proposals and finished commercials to clients for approval. A publisher will want to follow the status of a video game that is in development, and will need to approve hiring and budget decisions.

Therefore, the key for the creative team—and a small group of business counterparts—is to only allow such critical inputs, and to do so in a streamlined manner with short turnaround times. Avoid unnecessary requests, delays, and approvals that slow down or distract the team. Approve the budget, get legal sign-off, and move on.

Creative vs. business perspectives

Of course, "unnecessary" is a subjective term.

Consider the creative team behind a new website design. The team, which includes editors and designers, wants to present a clean, uncluttered layout to site visitors.

However, the sales team may look at the design and think about opportunities to monetize the white space with advertising. I've heard ad salespeople at news websites insist that allowing blank real estate on a web page is "like leaving money on the table." This is despite the fact that almost no one clicks on the additional ads, the extra boxes and links slow down loading times, and site visitors are infuriated by the distractions. From the sales team's perspective, though, it's a necessary change. One has only to look at the typical front page of a major news website to see how pervasive this attitude is—the jumble of ads, pop-up subscription reminders, and click-bait "partner content" is astonishing.

So, who is right? Keep in mind that making media audiences love flows from the creative team building the intangible hooks, not from the business team trying to squeeze a fraction of a cent from each additional page view. Unreasonable or nonessential demands made by business executives and other stakeholders can reduce those intangible qualities that are so essential to audience bonding.

Returning to the "money on the table" example, it's been repeatedly demonstrated that websites cluttered with distracting sign-up forms, autoplay video, and other slow-loading advertising elements are more likely to turn off site visitors, which in turn negatively impacts impressions, signups, and other metrics valued by media businesses. The following chart shows the impact of website loading delays on audience engagement for a subscription-based news website, FT.com. Subscribers whose pages took an additional three seconds to load read nearly 8% fewer articles over a four-week period compared to a control group who had normal site-loading times.

Delay	1 week	4 weeks
1 second	−4.9%	−4.6%
2 seconds	−4.4%	−5.0%
3 seconds	−7.2%	−7.9%

Source: FT.com

Similarly, a film, album, TV show, or video game that is bogged down by approvals and uninformed creative demands will lead to delays that not only result in wasted time and higher costs, but may also risk the success of the project if it fails to resonate with audiences. For example, cable TV networks are stuffing more and more ads into its programming, which alienates viewers and is associated with lower ratings. My personal peeve is product placement in sitcoms and other programs—it is so pervasive, and can ruin the sense of imagination and escape that one typically feels when watching a great program.

Ultimately, if creative teams are allowed to follow their visions with a minimum of unnecessary interference, business success will be far easier to achieve. Truly irresistible media sets up favorable business conditions, leading to higher demand (and higher prices) for tickets, downloads, ads, and subscriptions. Having Lean Media ideals flow from the top of the organization will go a long way toward getting everyone on board.

The role of marketing in a Lean Media project

When discussing stakeholder constituencies, there is one group that deserves a special mention: Marketing. Adopting Lean Media means moving away from the chubby mindset and extensive launch planning, which will have an impact on the role of the people responsible for marketing the work.

In certain sectors of the media industry, such as film and gaming, marketing considerations figure prominently in getting a project approved, which means senior marketing people will have a seat at the creative table from start to finish. Under Lean Media, marketing may have some influence during the ideation stage, but the original idea will likely undergo massive, rapid change as the creativity is focused and audience feedback starts to influence development. There will be a lot of uncertainty about the final product and the timeline for the flex launch. This makes it difficult to coordinate specific marketing elements, including promotions, advertising, and press coverage.

This does not mean the marketing team should disappear. Indeed, there is an opportunity for marketing to play a critical role in a Lean Media production—namely, recruiting and engaging test audiences. As we will see in chapters 7 and 8, identifying audiences and gathering feedback are significant challenges. Assigning the marketing group to take on these tasks will not only free up the creative team to concentrate on its work, but will also result in more effective marketing, thanks to a better understanding of the audience.

Note that the creative team cannot completely hand over the reins to marketing when it comes to working with audience feedback. The marketing group can help analyze the data, and may even have some interesting ideas about how to improve the media based on the quantitative and qualitative feedback. But it is really up to the creative team to digest what test audiences are telling them, and make changes based on the insights they glean.

Takeaways

- Take the opportunity at an early stage to communicate Lean Media principles to business executives, partners, investors, and other stakeholders. Focus on common ground and shared benefits, such as shortening development time, reducing the risk of failure, and creating great media that audiences love.

- Manage expectations to make it clear that the creative team will highly value feedback from test audiences, while feedback from executives, partners, and other stakeholders will rarely be solicited.

- Eliminate waiting times associated with approvals. On-the-spot decisions are better than saying "get back to me next week."

- Designate a buffer to handle questions and requests from outside the creative core. This person needs to be a senior staff (or team) member and should prevent the rest of the team from being unnecessarily distracted or influenced.

- When it is time to present media to stakeholders, the creative team needs to emphasize the shared goal of creating great media that audiences love. If necessary, present supporting evidence from test audiences, such as comments or quantitative data.

- Marketing people will be less involved in long-term planning, and more involved in helping gather feedback from test audiences.

CHAPTER 7

Lean Media audiences

Though I have worked in media for decades, it never ceases to amaze me how insulated creative teams are from their audiences. I know journalists, musicians, TV producers, website designers, and authors who rarely interact with the people who experience the media they create.

The reasons for doing so are varied. Some don't know how to connect with audiences. It's too difficult, or someone else (marketing, customer service, retailers, or a partner) controls the relationship. Others don't want to reach out to audiences, or claim they don't need to—quantitative data such as TV ratings, reader surveys, and website traffic logs supposedly give them all the insights that they need.

Examples abound. In recent years, news coverage and polling prior to national elections has completely underestimated or ignored large segments of the population, which has led to surprise electoral outcomes in Britain, the United States, and elsewhere. The data was wrong or incomplete, and the failure of the news media was compounded by selective bias on the part of journalists and Beltway political experts. The situation will not change until better sources of data are developed, and journalists get out of their offices in expensive megacities and make an effort to connect with everyday people in rural states and provinces.

I, too, have been guilty of not knowing my audience. For the first two years I worked for IDG, I never met a member of our magazine's readership. I thought I knew a little bit about them thanks to the articles and columns I helped edit, but it led to an incomplete (and inaccurate) picture of who our audience really was. In the newsrooms I worked in, 95% of the work took place in front of a computer or on the phone. Usually it was only the reporters who talked with sources.

After a promotion, my boss paid for me to attend one of our branded reader conferences held at a resort in Arizona. It was a fantastic opportunity to finally meet some of our readers. I could learn about them—what they did for a living, what mattered to them in terms of career development, and even what they liked to do for fun. I asked them what they thought about the product I was working on—a blogging community—and could take back some of the feedback to my team. After that experience, I made a point of going to as many reader conferences as possible.

I also made a point of going out into the field. Sometimes I accompanied reporters to help them cover stories, while at other times I went solo to conduct interviews or tour IT facilities. I met CIOs, CTOs, and other executives, as well as the lower-level IT staff who kept the data centers and software running. Once I toured a local police department, and learned how the head of IT extended computing technology to police cruisers and detectives. At a visit to a data center in New Jersey, I remember one of the staff lifting up a floor panel, revealing thick braids of Ethernet cable nearly two feet deep. It was through these visits that I truly began to understand the working environments of our target readers and some of the day-to-day challenges they faced, from purchasing laptops to updating the cooling systems in data centers. These experiences informed my writing, my use of sources and photos, and the questions I asked when I interviewed people.

Going beyond audience metrics

Media creators must go out and interact with their audiences in some meaningful way—scanning a reader survey or ratings report simply won't cut it. Making the effort to interact with audience members can help you understand their needs and make media that is more likely to resonate.

Creators in certain niches have no choice but to listen closely to their audiences and iterate. If they fail to do so, their creations will almost certainly fall flat. Comedians are natural Lean Media practitioners, using feedback from every show to pick the best bits and hone their delivery for the next performance.

When we see top comedians effortlessly performing on television or in a Las Vegas auditorium, it's natural to assume they were born with the ability to make people laugh. Certainly, many were known as class clowns or gifted storytellers while growing up. Looking into their career development, however, it's apparent that close contact with audiences over many years has enabled them to develop their on-stage personalities and improve their gags.

For instance, Amy Schumer was an experienced stage actress before giving stand-up comedy a try in 2004. She spent years on the club circuit before getting her break on the television show *Last Comic Standing*. Since then, she has developed stand-up routines and television programming focused on her awkward (and brutally honest) experiences with sex and relationships. Her core audience is dominated by young women, who find her humor irresistible. Like many great comedians, she uses live performances to test new bits, improve her timing, and develop other parts of the routine. When a joke falls flat or goes too far, she will make adjustments accordingly.

Some film studios now use focus groups as a way to improve storytelling and reduce the risk of failure. Marvel reportedly removed a scene featuring actor Tom Hiddleston from one of the movies in *The Avengers* series because it confused the plot among test audiences.

For people who are used to working with quantitative data, as well as those introverted creators who would prefer to spend all day sitting in front of a computer screen or working in the studio, going out and talking with human beings may be an uncomfortable thought. But I believe such contact is absolutely necessary to understand audiences on a deeper level. Meeting someone face-to-face reveals expressions, gestures, and various intangible reactions. A dialogue can help you understand who they are, what they do, and how they consume media.

Of course, not all media generates observable reactions. For instance, a reader of a book doesn't talk or do much of anything else while reading text. Once the book is finished, the reader will close the cover, put it back into the bookshelf, and move on.

However, ask an author what happens when he or she does a book signing or a live reading. Fans can be surprisingly animated—they will tell the author about their favorite titles or characters, ask questions about sequels and inspirations, and generally give the author lots of opportunities to better understand what makes them tick. There is also a long tradition in the book world of authors connecting with readers through the written word. Fifty or 100 years ago it was through letters. Nowadays it may be through email, social media, or online comments.

Leveraging technology to connect with audiences

Meeting audiences in person may be impractical for certain creators. An author or musician who works in the sticks may find it difficult to connect with fans (or potential fans) in person. The Vietnamese game designer who creates mobile games for the profitable North American market cannot easily meet young gamers in Canada or the U.S. She may also be restricted connecting directly with players, because gaming platforms usually don't share customers' contact info.

In such cases, the solution lies in technology. Notch, the developer behind Minecraft, lives in Sweden yet was able to remotely gather both quantitative and qualitative feedback about prototypes. He looked at hard quantitative data, such as growth in user signups to time spent in the virtual world. He paid close attention to gameplay data gathered from the test versions of the games. But Notch also kept a close eye on the qualitative online chatter about the early Minecraft builds on Internet discussion forums and YouTube comments. He also watched local gamers play Minecraft in person. In aggregate, this feedback helped him make decisions about the design of Minecraft, customization options, and the user interface.

It's not just game designers who can leverage technology to connect with audiences. Many writers have discovered the importance of developing an "author platform," or a digitally connected fan base. This entails creating a blog or fan website, building an email list to share news and book updates, and conversing with readers on Facebook, Goodreads, and Wattpad, an online community for sharing unreleased fiction. Through these channels, it is possible to connect with individual fans and gather feedback about new projects.

Audience targeting

Who is your audience? This is a simple question, yet the answers can be quite complex.

For instance, do you have an existing audience from a past project or current partnership? Would they be interested in the new media creation you are working on, or do you need to recruit a completely new audience? Is your audience homogenous, having the same general characteristics (e.g., college-educated single females aged 25–34)? Or can the audience be separated into distinct groups?

Many assume the audience for American football consists mostly of boys and men. Indeed, throughout the NFL season, male television viewership dominates female viewership 66% to 34%. However, during the Super Bowl, the demographics shift to 47% female viewers. This change shows the dynamic attributes of an audience.

Let's say you have a dedicated fan base from your earlier work. Some are old fans who have been following you since the beginning. Others may be new fans who only came on board last year, and they don't see eye to eye with the

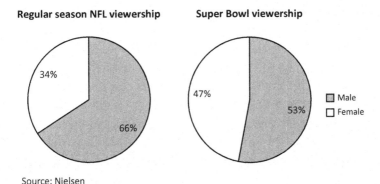

Regular season NFL viewership   **Super Bowl viewership**

34%

66%

47%

53%

☑ Male
☐ Female

Source: Nielsen

old fans. Another scenario: Fans in one market (Miami) behave quite differently than the ones in another (Beijing).

Audiences can change, too. The Beatles in the early 1960s were a talented boy band with identical haircuts and a knack for writing hook-filled R&B hits with great harmonies. The American fan base consisted of screaming teens as well as young shop clerks and office workers, many of whom were female. By the late 60s, The Beatles had grown out their hair and were writing hard rock, folk music, psychedelic songs, and experimental compositions. The boy band audience faded away, and were replaced by students, college-educated people in their 20s, and counterculture types, both male and female.

The takeaway here is audiences are not static, monolithic groups of people. In a Lean Media context, this needs to be taken into consideration when planning a new project and reaching out to test audiences.

Recruiting audiences for a Lean Media project

Recruiting test audiences is a task that fills many creators with dread. It requires interacting with real people outside of the comforts of the office or studio. Hard questions will need to be asked—how would they rate an idea or prototype? How does the media in question make them feel? What aspects work, and what rubs them the wrong way? Would they choose to experience the media again, or recommend it to someone?

Many creative people are only too happy to pass off the time-consuming tasks associated with recruiting and interacting with test audiences to a different group, such as marketing. This is an appropriate solution for creative teams, as it reduces wasted time and lets the team focus its efforts on making media. Marketing people also have real expertise dealing with audiences, and know how to reach out to testers, set up focus groups, conduct interviews, and create surveys.

What if there is no marketing group, or the creative team doesn't have the resources to hire someone to deal with test audiences? The team will have to work with testers on its own. As someone who manages a small publishing company with only limited outside marketing help, I can attest to the difficulties associated with finding test audiences for new books and other media. In some cases, I have been able to turn to existing fans and ask them to serve as beta readers or otherwise help evaluate a new work. But in the early days, before I had any readers, I had to get feedback using online tools or wait until the flex launch to see what audiences thought.

When it comes to online tools, the advent of social media, online forums, and low-cost online advertising has been a boon to small media teams seeking feedback. As a solo founder, I can spend a few hundred dollars for a short Google AdWords or Facebook advertising campaign to determine which version of a book cover people click on most or which title they prefer. These self-service ad platforms are relatively easy to use, and can help fledgling media ventures as well as solo creators gather crucial feedback from test audiences.

Tim Ferriss, the author and podcaster famed for his focus on productivity, famously tested a dozen versions of the title of his first book using a $200 Google AdWords campaign. His goal: to see which title resonated the most with audiences. By comparing the click-through rates of the different ads, he was able to determine which one had the highest response. "The Four-Hour Work-week" beat out titles like "Broadband and White Sand," and the rest is history!

However, it is a mistake to assume technology is a sure-fire way to recruit test audiences. Writers, game designers, videographers, and other media creators are competing for audiences' time and attention in an extremely crowded media landscape. At the very least, creators will need to employ clever tactics to identify and connect with potential audiences. But creators may also have to spend real time and money to get eyeballs on landing pages and online survey forms. At the end of the day, old-fashioned face-to-face audience interactions may be a more productive way to find and cultivate test audiences.

Can test audiences be trusted?

There is a good deal of skepticism surrounding test audiences. How can a handful of people recruited to check out a storyboard or listen to a demo track be considered a statistically valid representation? Even in a Hollywood focus group, where scores or even hundreds of people might watch the prerelease version of a new film or TV show, directors may question the opinions gleaned from the focus sessions. Half of the people in the groups are wannabe film critics, while the other half are liable to say something fawning or outrageous to please the film people, or so the thinking goes.

Turning to a relatively small group of people to vet an idea or look at a prototype is not ideal. But it is still possible to get useful insights, even if there are only a handful of people. If you show the rough cut of a supposedly hilarious car commercial to five people and no one cracks a smile, it's an indication that something may be wrong with the gag, the delivery, or the actors. Similarly, if every single person in your 10-person test group who tries out your mobile game prototype asks to play it again, that is an encouraging sign that you are on to something special.

For decades, author Stephen King has turned to a small group of "ideal" readers, including his wife, to give feedback on his manuscripts. In a magazine essay describing how he worked with his beta group, he wrote that if two or more people raise the same concern about a character, plot twist, snatch of dialogue, or some other element, it's necessary to change it, even if he liked it. However, if each beta reader is critical of something different, then their feedback can be disregarded, he said.

King's approach also brings up the issue of using friends and family members to provide feedback. There are definite advantages to turning to people you know. They are more accessible and will probably agree to take part. But there are drawbacks, too:

- Close family members may not be comfortable giving harsh feedback, or may exaggerate what they like about the work.

- Friends and family may not be true audience members—they would never watch, read, play, listen to, or otherwise experience the media in question, and are only volunteering as a personal favor to the creators.

- Because it is so easy to fall back on friends and family, it may be tempting to avoid reaching out to strangers.

For these reasons, I advise limiting the numbers of friends and family giving feedback. The creative team (and/or their marketing colleagues) must make an effort to connect with outside test audiences. And, if a friend or family member does volunteer to give feedback, make sure he or she really belongs to the target audience—while great aunt Ursula may be a suitable beta reader for a mystery novel, she would not be able to give useful insights about a new EDM track you're working on.

Test pods

Every media team should have access to a group of reliable and conscientious testers who can give qualitative or quantitative feedback when the need arises. I call this group a test pod. If you build the pod in advance, it can yield valuable insights when feedback is required during production. Furthermore, it is possible to return to this group again and again as the project progresses or even use the pod across different projects.

Members should be chosen with care. You want people who not only belong to the target audience, but are also so interested in the media being produced that they are willing to take time from their crowded schedules to share their views.

The pod does not have to be big, but should have enough members to generate a range of insights for each feedback session. A test pod with 20 to 30 members will be ideal, but this number can be smaller if the venture is new (and therefore unknown to potential recruits) or it takes a lot of time to evaluate prototypes (which excludes people who don't have much spare time).

Opportunities to recruit test pods
Audience members at signings/public appearances
Audience members who have initiated contact in the past
Email newsletter recipients
Extended network
Fan clubs
Fans of past works
Google AdWords campaigns
Media interview audiences
Notices at libraries, theaters, or other media venues
Social media advertisements
Social media followers
Website appeals

Elizabeth Turnbull of Light Messages, a North Carolina-based trade publisher, uses a test pod to evaluate incoming manuscript submissions. The pod includes a half-dozen dedicated fans of Light Messages authors who have agreed to serve as beta readers for new books by other authors. Turnbull and her colleagues will do the first round of manuscript vetting. Light Messages will then distribute the manuscripts that have potential to the test pod and ask for their qualitative feedback. Their input helps the publisher determine whether or not to make offers to the manuscripts' authors.

Surrogate audiences

Regardless of whether they use Lean Media methods or not, media pros frequently rely on surrogate audiences to understand the market for new media.

Surrogate audiences are groups of people who like media that's similar to what you are working on. Let's say you are producing a new TV show, *Rodent World*, which explores the fascinating lives of squirrels, mice, rabbits, and chipmunks. People who follow an existing program on another network called *Extreme Rodents* represent a surrogate audience. An understanding of what makes them tick may help your team as you build out *Rodent World*.

Or, if you are developing a new subscription-based website about mutual funds, you could turn to the audience of one of your earlier websites that covered the stock market. There is an assumption that if people liked your previous work, then surely, they (or people like them) will become fans of whatever new, similar work you are developing.

When media people say, "I understand audiences" or "I know what the public wants" they are actually referring to surrogate audiences, as opposed to an established audience of an existing work. There are even a small number of experienced media professionals—people of the caliber of filmmaker Steven Spielberg, reality television producer Mark Burnett, or graphic designer Paula Scher—who are so in touch with surrogate audiences' tastes and their own teams' creative talents that they are able to crank out a seemingly nonstop string of hits over periods of many decades. Music executive L.A. Reid, who helped produce and/or develop a long string of artists including TLC, Avril Lavigne, Justin Bieber, Rihanna, and Meghan Trainor, calls himself a "superconsumer" who knows and respects the tastes of the music-listening public. The Reids and Spielbergs of the world have a sixth sense for understanding the intangible elements that audiences desire, and are able to craft media that satisfies them.

Surrogate audiences are an attractive alternative to using test audiences or market research. They remove a lot of guesswork about audience preferences and behavior. Often, surrogate audiences can illustrate trends or point the way to an audience hit.

Some readers may remember *The Monkees*, a mid-60s TV sitcom about a hapless Los Angeles pop band. The Monkees was a manufactured band, devised by

TV executives and recruited by Hollywood talent scouts. The idea was inspired by a growing interest in rock music. The surrogate audience consisted of millions of young people who listened to easygoing pop bands such as The Beach Boys and Herman's Hermits and laughed at the goofy Beatles film *A Hard Day's Night*. While the members of The Monkees could all play instruments, they never built up a grassroots following by playing clubs, touring, or self-recording singles for the radio. For the first two years, they didn't even write their own music—they simply played tunes that had been written for them by studio professionals.

The Hollywood entertainment executives who devised *The Monkees* took a gamble by assuming the surrogate audience—fans of real mid-60s pop bands— would like the fake band presented on television. They were right. The tunes were catchy, the TV scripts were good, and the four actors clicked. Audiences loved them. *The Monkees* became such a sensation that the music eventually overshadowed the TV show, with recording and touring continuing after the TV series had ended.

Another example of surrogate audiences leading to success involves the craze for adult coloring books. It was a bizarre idea that enjoyed success in the 1960s as a mildly subversive pastime, then exploded once again in the early teens following the release of Johanna Basford's *Secret Garden* and several other titles released by European publishers. Buyers liked the nostalgic and soothing themes, and publishers and illustrators in other countries took notice. Many were rewarded for their efforts, with tens or even hundreds of thousands of units sold. The adult coloring books category was cited as one of the reasons overall printed book sales experienced a recovery in the United States in 2015.

Making assumptions based on surrogate audiences carries significant risks, though. Maybe it is difficult to market to a surrogate audience, because another media entity controls the audience. Or perhaps the new media does not reso-nate because the field is too crowded. For instance, news websites that have tried to mimic *The Huffington Post* and *Buzzfeed* have found that audiences are hard to connect with because the leaders are well-established and there is too much free news available online.

Another scenario in which surrogate assumptions can backfire: Audiences don't care for the new product because the intangible qualities that made the original so great are not present in the versions that come later. Hollywood is famous for producing sequels that don't have the magic of the original (*Jurassic Park III*, anyone?) or are poor "me-too" clones that simply are not special. Bands often worry about the "sophomore slump," so-called because of the tendency of second albums failing to live up to audience expectations after an exceptional debut effort.

Then there is the problem of audiences moving on. Atari and Chuck E. Cheese founder Nolan Bushnell was once asked about mistakes he had made in his entrepreneurial career. "I didn't understand the nature of entertainment," he said. "Entertainment is very fragile. It's driven on novelty," he explained, pointing to the example of huge turnouts for a new product or entertainment craze that quickly faded away.

There are many other examples of this phenomenon. Rapper MC Hammer was one of the hottest performers of the early 1990s, but his parachute pants and huge dance troupes quickly fell out of favor as audiences turned to harder-edged rap. MC Hammer's subsequent attempt to reinvent himself as a "gangster rapper" failed. Similarly, the craze for vampire-themed TV shows and books peaked around 2011 and faded as teen audiences turned to *The Hunger Games* and other dystopian fiction. Angry Birds was the hot mobile game of 2010, but a few years later it was difficult to get audiences excited about sequels, much less *Angry Birds Movie* which was released in the summer of 2016 and failed to reinvigorate the brand.

Finally, a big problem with making assumptions based on surrogate audiences is it gives short shrift to the creative soul of the team. Producing media turns into an exercise of copying other ideas or returning to the same formula that worked the last time. Certainly, there is an expectation of continuity in serial media or follow-up efforts. But trying to please surrogate audiences often leads to lackluster creative efforts that are drab and uninspiring.

Checking outside of your target audience

People who are not in your target audience can still provide value—if chosen with care. These outside audiences need to have a connection with the target audience and/or must relate to some element of the media being created.

For instance, in 2016 Red Chair Press launched Scary Tales Retold, a series of horror-themed fairy tales for readers ages 6 through 9. The books tried to tread a fine line between being funny and scary. Titles included *Cinderella and the Vampire Prince, Jack and the Bloody Beanstalk*, and *Goldilocks and the Three Ghosts*. I spoke with publisher Keith Garton, who described two groups of beta readers: kids and parents. The kids liked the concept, and giggled at the outrageous scenarios, such as Cinderella becoming a vampire.

While parents were not in the target audience, Red Chair Press knew they would be buying the books and would be sensitive to books that are too scary for their children. When it came to feedback from adults, parents were concerned that the books were inappropriate for younger children, and the age range of the books needed to be clearly stated on the cover.

Another reason for a Lean Media practitioner to pay attention to people who are not in the target audience is they may turn out to be an actual audience in the future. Until the early 2000s, many in the video game industry assumed the "gamer" audience consisted only of young males. Now it is clear that games can appeal to young and old of both sexes. Game designers may think they are creating media that targets a specific demographic group, such as male college students. But if a test of the prototype with people from other groups reveals that women aged 18 to 34 also enjoy the game, maybe it's time for the creative team to include this other audience in the feedback loops and ask the marketing team to expand advertising campaigns to include young women.

Similarly, when *The Simpsons* was first aired as bumpers in *The Tracey Ullman Show*, media writers probably assumed the ideal audience member was the same type of person who would watch Ullman—a young adult who liked sketch comedy. Once *The Simpsons* was repurposed as a standalone half-hour prime time program, it became apparent that the program had much wider appeal, from kids to senior citizens. With slapstick jokes for the kids and obscure pop culture, political, and historical references for the adults, *The Simpsons* was a program that went beyond Ullman's narrow niche.

There is another interesting use of non-target audiences, which I call the anti-audience. This approach involves surveying people who are the opposite of the target audience in terms of their tastes and preference. By understanding what the anti-audience likes, you will thereby gain insights into what your true audience *dislikes*, and vice versa.

Carlton "Chuck D" Ridenhour of the outspoken rap band Public Enemy used this technique by playing demo versions of Public Enemy songs to his girlfriend (and future wife). If there was a song that she particularly liked, Ridenhour would remove it from the album. His reasoning: If she liked it, it meant the song was too "soft" for Public Enemy's target audience. Conversely, if she hated the song, that was something that had serious potential.

Takeaways

- Creators need to understand audiences on more than a superficial level. This may require going beyond reading summary metrics or demographic reports, and actually interacting with audience members.

- Recruit test pods, consisting of prospective audience members who are willing to give feedback on a sustained basis.

- Surrogate audiences are groups of people who like media that's similar to your own project. They are an alternative to test audiences, but can lead to boring or copycat creations.

LEAN
MEDIA

CHAPTER 8

Leveraging feedback for Lean Media

Creative teams have used feedback to develop and hone media since ancient times. In the margins of celebrated paintings from the Chinese dynastic era, one can see the annotations left by other learned masters who shared their opinions and praise. Shakespeare paid attention to the opinions of collaborators and patrons. In more recent times, members of The Beatles sought feedback from each other, as well as from producer George Martin, manager Brian Epstein, record label executives, and music industry peers.

These types of professional feedback can still be seen in the industry today, and can be categorized according to their impact and source:

Major impact:

- **Internal.** Members of the core creative team give each other feedback as the work is developed.

- **Stakeholder.** Includes internal stakeholders such as senior executives and colleagues in different business units, as well as external stakeholders such as investors, clients, and partner firms.

Minor impact:

- **Peer.** This category includes creators who might be known to the core team (such as a mentor, former colleague, or a friend with a similar background) or other creators who are somehow exposed to the media through performances, news coverage, award programs, etc.

- **Media.** Critics, columnists, bloggers, YouTubers, trade publications, and trusted industry observers still play an important publicity role for new media. However, their impact on creators may be limited. Creators often disdain critical reviews. Further, few will admit tailoring media to gain approval from professional critics.

Qualitative and quantitative audience feedback

Outside of professional feedback sources, feedback from audiences play a role in traditional media. As noted earlier, the impact is limited or nonexistent during the production stages. All too often, the creative team will not know what audiences will think of the production until after the public launch.

The shift to digital media has led to an explosion of data. Internet comments and reviews written by audience members are obvious examples of qualitative feedback, but creators can also dig a little deeper with online surveys and comment forms.

At one time, quantitative data was limited to sales data or surveys, such as Nielsen ratings for broadcast television. In recent years, quantitative data has greatly expanded as the industry has moved to digital platforms. It now includes demographic information, platform usage, social shares and likes, return visitors, and even the drop-off points where people stop watching a video program or reading a book.

The games industry employs quantitative tools that are capable of measuring feeling. "Some teams take video of test group players' faces as they play and sync to [gameplay] data so they can infer emotion," states video game executive Don Daglow. "The emotional feedback is a subset of users but can still be really helpful." Daglow believes that having the digital tools to measure feeling holds an advantage over written surveys or interviews, because what gamers say may be different from how they actually behave.

"In my humble opinion, creativity drives but analytics is riding shotgun," he says. "We used to ship games and pray they worked well. Now we ship games and we have tools to help us tune them until they work great. We need to start with a clear vision, but I love the great feedback we get if and when we ask the right questions."

How traditional media uses professional feedback

Traditional media companies that take a chubby approach prefer professional feedback from two sources: the core creative team and stakeholders (internal as well as external). The feedback from these groups tends to be qualitative.

For example, a creative team working on a new entertainment website will discuss among themselves what's working and what's not. The comments might be broad suggestions ("I think we should avoid publishing critical articles") or detailed directives ("increase the vertical line spacing on the front page").

At various points in the production process, the team will show design mockups and sample pages to internal stakeholders such as the CEO and sales team. The feedback from the CEO might include approval or rejection of certain designs, or broad directives to bring out a certain element ("we need better headlines," or "can the site navigation include a link to our email newsletter?"). The sales team will be concerned about the appeal of the site to advertising clients, and the placement and functionality of various ad units.

External stakeholders will also get a chance to see the progress of the design and site content. Their feedback will be passed along to the creative team. For instance, investors might say what they like about the designs but may also have the power to reject certain elements. Advertising partners might pass their opinions back to the sales team, who will be eager to satisfy their wishes in order to close a business deal. The feedback may be technical ("the right rail will need to be widened to work with our preferred ad unit") or relate to the design and editorial focus of the site, which may be tricky to navigate—what a sales client wants may conflict with the core team's creative vision or what audience members want.

Other types of professional feedback will have a limited impact. In certain cases, a member of the core team may show the designs to a peer prior to launch. The feedback will be qualitative and critical. The lead designer of the online entertainment site may show wireframes to an old colleague or mentor, or ask a classmate from design school about appropriate color palettes and fonts for this type of site. While the creative team may be willing to implement minor suggestions from their peers, major changes are unlikely for a number of reasons, including professional pride and the potential for creative input requiring public credit and/or a cut of the proceeds.

Critics, bloggers, and reporters may also be given access to the media prior to launch for review or interview purposes. However, their feedback will typically not be made available until just before or right after the launch. Further, media critics are only given access to final or near-final versions in order to support the marketing plan and raise awareness, as opposed to helping the core creative team improve the product.

In a Lean Media setting, there will be two major changes in the impact of various feedback constituencies: Non-creative stakeholders (both internal and external) will have a lesser impact, while the influence of audience feedback will grow. The following diagram illustrates the dynamics:

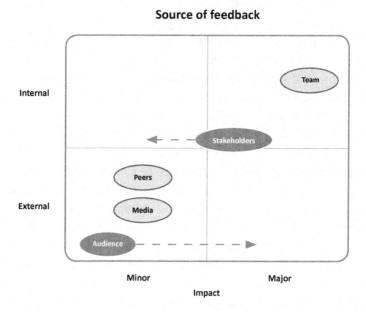

Source of feedback

The problem with stakeholder feedback

As mentioned earlier, during the production process for a traditional media company, test audiences are unlikely to experience the media or give feedback to the creative team. This means a corporate sales rep, media investor, or an executive from a partner organization will potentially have a greater impact on the creative development of the media than actual members of the target audience!

That's not to say that professional feedback is useless. Sometimes valid or important observations will be made by stakeholders. But along with a few promising ideas will come a lot of wrong assumptions and misguided advice.

A classic mistake involves subjective bias—the assumption that one's own preferences are shared by the audience, even if the stakeholder giving feedback is not a member of the target audience.

Another issue: mission creep, as stakeholders add on more creative and technical requirements that delay the project and distract the team.

Stakeholders may also pass along self-serving feedback which, if implemented, can potentially harm a media project. This was discussed in Chapter 6, but it's worth revisiting. In a nutshell, the goals of stakeholders may not be closely aligned with the goals of the creative team or the interests of the target audience. A sales rep ultimately needs to keep his or her clients happy and maximize commissions. An investor seeks a return on his or her capital in the form of dividends or the sale of the company.

In contrast, the creative team will be trying to achieve a creative vision and produce media that audiences love. Individual audience members consume media in order to satisfy various intangible needs. If the sales team's feedback centers on increasing the visibility of advertising, it potentially forces the creative team to make design compromises elsewhere. If the feedback results in an advertising unit that takes over the entire screen, audiences will not stick around.

Audience metrics

For many traditional media releases, creative and business teams don't see any audience feedback until after the launch. While creators will be interested in qualitative feedback from audience members, the business team (and external stakeholders) will want to get their hands on quantitative data that tracks popularity and sales. The data includes:

TV & Radio: Broadcast ratings are provided by Nielsen. In recent years, there has been a shift to monitoring digital downloads and digital streams.

Film: Box office figures are important during the initial launch. Digital downloads, DVD sales, and streams are important later in the film's life cycle.

Songs: In the old days, album sales and *Billboard* magazine's singles and album charts ruled the music world. Since the early 2000s, there has been a shift to tracking digital downloads and streaming music.

Books: Publishers follow retail sales as well as ebook downloads. Retailers can track annual purchases by various customer segments, and can also identify titles that are often bought together with other titles. Nielsen-owned services track retail sales data as well as ISBN registrations in the United States. The following diagram, provided by Amazon to authors, shows the number of books sold through retail channels in one week in specific metropolitan areas. Such data can inform future marketing campaigns and book tours.

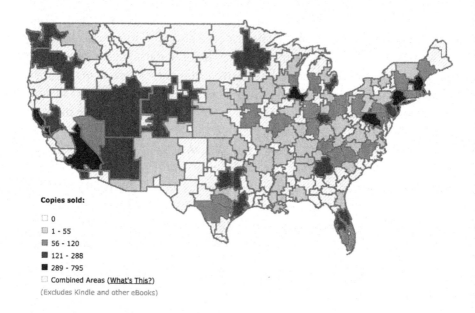

Copies sold:

☐ 0
▥ 1 - 55
▨ 56 - 120
■ 121 - 288
■ 289 - 795
☐ Combined Areas (What's This?)
(Excludes Kindle and other eBooks)

Newspapers & magazines: While print media has been decimated by digital competition, subscriber and circulation numbers are still used to gauge audience interest and establish advertising rates.

Websites: Successful sites tout pageviews, unique visitors, and audience demographics gleaned through surveys or other means. However, there is also an interest in tracking engagement, which might include time spent on site, the number of pages per visitor, comments, "likes," and social shares.

Video games: Metrics vary by platform. For console games, studios track the sale of physical media as well as downloads. Mobile game developers track installations, daily or monthly active users, in-game purchases, and progression metrics. Tools to measure emotional reactions are also gaining ground at some of the larger studios.

Advertising: Traditional print and broadcast advertising has long been hobbled by imperfect metrics—it's difficult to determine how many people look at a newspaper advertisement or watch a TV commercial. The advent of digital advertising has opened new possibilities for gathering quantitative feedback, demographic data, and conversion rates.

How do business teams use quantitative data? Positive data can serve as a cue to expand distribution or start planning a sequel. Negative data can result in a rejiggered marketing campaign or minor changes to creative elements, such as tweaking the title of a movie or changing the cover of a book. Media companies also employ tactics that can boost long tail, midlist, or foreign sales.

However, if the quantitative and qualitative audience feedback is consistently negative, no amount of changes to the marketing or distribution will make the target audience come around. The investment in time, money, and other resources will have to be written off.

The lean approach to feedback

Creators using lean methods have a far different outlook when it comes to leveraging feedback compared to their counterparts taking the chubby launch approach. The three Lean Media principles—reduce waste, focus creativity, and understand audiences—shift the emphasis for certain types of feedback:

- Internal feedback will help focus creativity and drive development.

- Audience feedback is elevated to a position of prominence, per the principle of understanding audiences.

- Stakeholder feedback will play a reduced role, per the principle of reducing waste.

Two major feedback changes are the reduction in the number of stakeholder touchpoints and the incorporation of audience feedback cycles earlier into the development process. As discussed in Chapter 6, stakeholders will not appreciate their reduced influence, but there are approaches to managing the transition.

Deciding which elements require feedback often boils down to identifying specific areas that the team knows need improvement or involve uncertainty. Alternately, the team can present a complete or semi-complete version of the work, and see which elements generate feedback.

Not every creative decision requires audience feedback to move the project forward. In some cases, it may not be practical to gather feedback, or doing so would take too long. For other elements and ideas, members of the creative team will be confident in their vision and execution, and therefore do not need feedback from audiences.

Feedback at the Idea stage

Take a look at the Lean Media flowchart, introduced in Chapter 5:

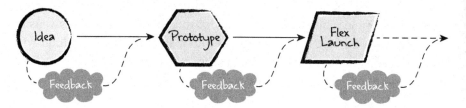

There are opportunities to gather audience feedback at every stage of the production, starting with the idea itself.

Let's say you are in an established band and are thinking about recording a new song or album. Under the traditional media model, this would be discussed by the members of the core team (the band and its creative associates) as well as stakeholders such as management and music industry executives. You might also bounce the idea off a few peers.

The Lean Media framework doesn't require the use of feedback at every stage of the production. But why not start with the idea? Even if you haven't recruited a test pod, it's easy enough to take a few members of the fan club out for a beer, and ask them about what they think of the next recording project. Or, post an anonymous message to the fan club bulletin board and ask the same question.

The goal is not to determine how many fans give their stamps of approval. As creators, you are not looking for permission from fans to move forward. You are also not looking for specific song ideas—that will come from the songwriters on the team. Rather, the purpose of talking with audience members at this early stage is to try to understand where they are coming from vis à vis the band's music and the next recording project.

The qualitative feedback will be varied. It will probably include unusual observations, repetitive praise, and contradictory advice. But you will also hear some useful insights that the team can bring back and discuss. Some insights may even lead to innovative ideas that allow the band to steer the creative focus in a new direction.

Consider the following comments:

- "I really liked the acoustic song at the end of the last album."

- "A new album? Didn't you just release one last year?"

- "When your bass player and drummer are really tight, it's awesome!"

- "Five years ago, I thought dance music was stupid, but then I went to an EDM show. Intense!"

- "I've got a new job so I can't go to shows on weekdays anymore."

- "New songs? Finally!"

- "The fans who have joined the club in the last year, they like the harder stuff more."

- "You could release an album of Madonna covers and I'd still love it."

Not all of these observations will be helpful. But they do give insights into what some audience members are thinking. There are also some intriguing possibilities derived from the feedback—producing an all-acoustic album, or recording songs that incorporate elements of electronic dance music. The band is not obliged to act, but the songwriters can certainly consider the ideas.

Scott Adams, the creator of the *Dilbert* syndicated comic series, leveraged test audiences and fans to develop characters, storylines, and other elements of the strip. *Dilbert* was developed while Adams still worked at an office job in California. One method of gathering early feedback involved drawing characters on a whiteboard in his office and asking coworkers for feedback. The name "Dilbert" actually comes from a "Name the Nerd" whiteboard challenge. His boss came up with the idea!

What if there are no fans?

It's a common scenario for new media ventures or a young team creating something for the first time to have a limited fan base. The members of a just-formed band, the producers of a proposed TV pilot, or an inexperienced game developer won't have fans to turn to.

That does not mean the situation is hopeless. The trick will be to determine the target audience(s) and then identify people who fit the bill and are willing to give feedback.

Most creators will have a good sense of who they are targeting. Regard the following examples:

- A new country & western band can safely assume their audience will include existing fans of country & western music. A surrogate audience can be used to narrow the focus, based on a small group of country & western bands with a similar sound to the newcomers.

- The agency designing an online advertising campaign for a new light pickup truck will know the demographics of the target audience based on data provided by the manufacturer's marketing department. They may also be directed to target certain geographical regions in line with regional dealerships' sales goals.

- The producers of a proposed reality television show about organic farmers will want to talk with consumers of organic produce. Such consumers are likely to range between the ages of 30 and 49, have higher-than-average earnings, and live in suburban and urban areas with high concentrations of organic produce markets.

- An inexperienced game developer will choose an audience that likes similar games to whatever he or she has in mind. A mobile word jumble game is likely to attract fans of other word jumble games (e.g., educated people aged 40 and above, skewing female) whereas a first-person shooter for the Xbox based on an alien invasion would attract a mostly male audience aged 14 to 25.

After identifying the target audience(s), it will be time to connect with a few testers. For the new country & western band, it will be easy. The members have listened to this type of music for years, and will know like-minded people who share their tastes. It won't be hard to reach out to them to discuss their new music project in terms that this audience will understand: "We're starting a new band that's like a cross between Kacey Musgraves and LoCash Cowboys. What do you think?"

However, connecting with audiences may be difficult if the creators don't have any existing ties to the target audience. For instance, if the producers of the proposed TV show about organic farmers have a farming background and live in a rural area, they may have a tough time finding members of their target audience—consumers of organic produce are more likely to live far away in an urban or suburban setting. In this situation, it may be necessary to visit an organic farmer's market in the nearest big city and strike up conversations with shoppers. Or, they could try to start a conversation online, using social media or an online forum dedicated to organic food.

Overcoming mental roadblocks to prototype feedback

At what point should test audiences be exposed to early prototypes? Ideally, the creators want to be able to show something that can generate relevant insights. However, there may not be enough material to show them at an early stage in the production. For a movie that has only just started shooting, a single scene will probably not be sufficient if it seems too disjointed. On the other hand, a single scene may be adequate to show off the talents of specific cast members or the charisma between the leading actors. For the director and other people on the creative team, an alternate approach to gather early feedback would be to show storyboards or scripts to test audiences.

Beyond the issue of what to show, there is also a psychological issue that relates to the creators themselves. Media professionals are generally reluctant to show rough versions of their work to anyone outside of the core team. There are several reasons for this:

Perfectionism. The director who insists on 23 takes for a minor scene. The website designer who tries scores of typefaces before making a decision. The author who spends years "tweaking" the manuscript before submitting it to the publisher. The creative head at the ad agency who insists on the team pulling a series of all-nighters before a client presentation. We've all run into media pros who obsess over details and look down at others whose standards aren't high enough. They have difficulty letting go of projects they feel aren't ready, and the thought of showing an unfinished prototype to test audiences is alarming to them.

Criticism. No one likes having their work criticized. Even experienced media people who are used to being in the public eye can be surprisingly thin-skinned when their work is picked apart by professional critics or members of the public. Social media has brought a flood of new critics to the fore, raising the potential for criticism to go viral.

Leaks. The music industry has obsessed about unauthorized leaks of songs, albums, and unauthorized concert recordings since the analog era. In the digital age, creators of other types of media worry about new works being leaked or pirated. In this kind of environment, sharing prototypes with test audiences could lead to the songs showing up on file-sharing networks within days, or crucial plot details of a superhero movie showing up on an Internet discussion board before the launch.

Some professionals might require regular sessions on the therapist's couch to work out such deep-seated fears. However, there are other ways to address these concerns.

Perfectionism is hard to square with Lean Media. After all, the framework requires creators to let test audiences see unfinished versions of the work, which by definition are far from perfect. There are, however, ways to make perfectionists more comfortable with the process.

For instance, it's possible to polish the segment or demo or manuscript before showing it to audiences. This is much easier to do nowadays, owing to the powerful technical tools available to even low-budget productions.

Take the film industry. In the old days, shooting film required expensive and time-consuming processes relating to developing the film and editing it. Nowadays, digital video rivals the quality of 35mm film and allows for instant playback. Editors can also turn to inexpensive professional editing software on a PC or Mac.

Another compelling reason to polish prototypes relates to the impact on test audiences. Technical or creative scaffolding such as notes, timecodes, counters,

A film editor using a PC-based editing suite.

and raw computer scripts are a nagging reminder of the incomplete nature of the prototype, and will obscure the creative elements that audiences need to experience. For this reason, when I show a draft copy of a manuscript to a test reader, I always remove tracking, comments, and other annotations. They are a major distraction and serve no useful purpose to testers.

As for criticism, everyone working in media has to deal with it throughout their careers. However, for the most experienced and high-profile creators, the criticism will be tougher because expectations are so high and there is a much larger audience paying attention.

The way to deal with criticism in a Lean Media context is to regard it as a tool for identifying problems and improving quality. It will also be easier to accept criticism from a small test audience than a large public audience.

Test audiences will behave differently, too. Assuming creative teams (or their marketing colleagues) have communicated to the testers that they are being presented with prototypes, these audiences will expect that things will be rough around the edges or incomplete. They may also feel special that they are getting a sneak peek. This makes it more likely that criticism will be constructive rather than dismissive.

Leaks are often the result of careless or resentful insiders who prematurely distribute samples to people who should not have access. If you are worried about test audiences sharing prototypes, the best course of action is to have them experience the media in a closed environment where it's difficult to copy or share. For instance:

- Password-protect the demo version of a website.

- Show test audiences a video or film in a screening room.

- Let game testers use your own device to play the prototype version.

Some media companies insist on non-disclosure agreements to prevent testers from publicly discussing a work in progress. However, the anonymous nature of the Internet and the costs associated with filing lawsuits makes it impractical to enforce NDAs. It is better to recruit test pods consisting of audience members who are serious about providing feedback, and communicating to them the importance of keeping quiet about what they have seen until the media is officially released. Try sweetening the deal with some benefit that lets them feel that they are getting something in return for their time, effort, and discretion, such as access to the creative team, free tickets or gift cards, or access to future testing sessions.

Making plans for collecting feedback

So the creative team has overcome its hang-ups about sharing prototypes with test audiences. It's time to gather feedback.

Before you reach out, you will need to plan several aspects of gathering feedback. The following questions can help frame the requirements:

What aspect(s) of the production are you seeking feedback on? It may be tempting to answer "everything," but is that necessary? There are situations in which only a certain element requires feedback. For instance, if you are preparing a regional advertising campaign for a new sports bar, perhaps you want to determine which visuals resonate the most with the target audience. Or, if you are working on a new televised comedy series, you might want to see how audiences react to a new member of the troupe.

How much time is required? It's much easier to ask someone for 20 minutes of his or her time than asking for 2 hours. When I was writing this book, I only asked a handful of beta readers to tackle the entire manuscript at a relatively late stage in the prototyping process. These were media professionals who were really interested in the topic and had volunteered to read the whole thing. At earlier stages, I only asked for feedback on individual chapters or portions of chapters that could be read relatively quickly.

How will the feedback be gathered? Whether you seek quantitative or qualitative information to bring back to the creative core, you will need to think through the questions that will be asked or the sources of data that will be tapped. Taking the earlier example of the online ad campaign for pickup trucks, there are two main approaches:

Face-to-face

- General approach: Meet with a small group of customers in your target audience (for instance, men aged 18 to 55 who are likely to buy a truck for work purposes or outdoor recreation in the next 3 years) and show them some sample visuals.

- Qualitative feedback: Ask prepared questions ("what do you like about design #3?") or start a free-form discussion ("why are midsized pickup trucks important in your life?"). Record the session or ask participants to write down their thoughts.

- Quantitative feedback: Ask participants to fill out a survey form and rate the designs on a ten-point scale.

Online

- General approach: Use social media, email, and paid search advertising to direct test audiences to a website that shows videos of pickup trucks being used for work, home use, and recreation.

- Qualitative feedback: Participants use an online form to share their thoughts about the designs.

- Quantitative feedback: Site metrics provide insights into use of navigation links, search boxes, and icon-activated features.

As you can imagine, there are pros and cons to each approach. For instance, online forms make it easier to gather data, but you may be missing an opportunity to ask spontaneous follow-up questions. And while quantitative data in the form of ratings allows for quick comparisons of distinctive designs, you may be missing some of the nuanced concerns that might come out of a qualitative Q&A session.

Note that other tools may be available, depending on the format and the resources available to the team. A British company, Jellybooks, has developed technology that lets publishers understand how test readers are consuming ebooks, and where readers are most likely to stop reading a story. Similar software tools can give insights into how people are consuming video games and mobile apps.

Soft launch feedback

Compared to the rough prototypes, the flex launch version will be highly polished. It will also be publicly available, regardless of whether it's a hard launch, soft launch, or staggered launch.

If the team decides to do a soft launch, audience exposure could be restricted to a small market or limited distribution channel. The purpose of the soft launch is to expose real audiences to a final or near final version of the media to see how they respond. The creative team will remain open to making changes based on audience feedback.

Earlier, I discussed Scott Adams' methods for testing ideas and prototypes on an office whiteboard. His flexible approach to *Dilbert* started after it entered syndication, but before the comic strip got really big. To solicit feedback and learn about his audience, Adams began to include his email address on one of the panels. He was soon inundated with thousands of messages from fans. Based on their feedback, he began to change certain aspects of the series, including:

The settings of the strip. Early in the series, before the email address was posted, Dilbert spent a lot of time at home, shopping, or outside. Fans emailed to say they liked Dilbert best when he was in the office. As a result, Adams began to work office settings into the strip on a more frequent basis.

Characters. Readers told Adams they liked the cat character. Someone even gave it a nam—"Catbert"—which Adams incorporated into the strip. He also decided to give Catbert a bigger role—the head of the human resources department! His reasoning: HR was a perfect role for Catbert because cats don't care what people think of them and like to play with their human owners.

For my small publishing company, I regard all book launches as *de facto* soft launches. I frequently make changes to books based on qualitative and quantitative feedback, and some of the changes are significant.

For example, *Spreadsheets In 30 Minutes* had extremely poor sales when it was first launched. It was so bad, I contemplated withdrawing the title from sale.

Quantitative feedback in the form of basic sales data and retail ranking indicated the problem was taking place at the point of sale. As prospective readers browsed the sales listing, did they find something wrong with the cover art, marketing description, price, or title? That did not seem likely—I had used similar cover art, marketing descriptions, and prices for other titles in the series, but those books still sold well.

That left the title. I decided to change it, experimenting with a few different versions before settling on *Excel Basics In 30 Minutes*. Within six months, sales picked up greatly, as people discovered the book through keyword searches and Amazon's "also bought" feature. As of this writing, the book is now the topseller in the In 30 Minutes catalog, and has sold well over 5,000 copies since the title change.

Filtering feedback and leveraging user personas

Not all feedback needs to be brought back to the creative team. The Lean Media principles that you need to be cognizant of in this context are understanding audiences and focusing creativity. Not every data point or comment from your test audience will be relevant, so it is up to you (or whoever is responsible for bringing the information back to the team) to zero in on what's important.

Let's say you work for a small game studio. You are responsible for analyzing some survey data relating to a new mobile game that pits the player against an army of mutant cockroaches. After having a group of 40 test players play through a level, you ask the testers which of the following titles has the most appeal:

1. Cockroach apocalypse

2. Cockroach invasion

3. Humans vs. cockroaches

4. No preference

Each option gets roughly 25% from the testers. It's possible to make two conclusions about the data:

• There is no clear winner among the listed names.

• Testers did not hate the names either (otherwise, "no preference" would have scored much higher).

The results do not need to be brought back to the rest of the team. If they are brought back, they can be disregarded, as they will not help the team in its discussions of the proposed titles. Instead, the team can debate among themselves about which title to use, without audience input.

As for the feedback that *does* make it back to the core team, even if it is not acted upon, it should at least be evaluated against where team members are trying to take their product or vision. What can the feedback tell the creators about the audience? Are there ideas or information that can be incorporated into subsequent iterations? In many cases, feedback may be contradictory, misleading, or at odds with the team's creative vision. But such feedback should nevertheless spark discussions, and ideally help the team focus their creativity.

Bede McCarthy, of the *Financial Times*, describes the lean processes his team uses to improve the next generation FT.com website as such: "We generally get conflicting feedback about everything," he says. What the team tries to do is zero in on themes, such as the elements or issues testers complain about most often, even if there happens to be some positive feedback about the same features. Another tool to filter and prioritize feedback are user personas—"a primary and secondary who capture the two types of customer we are working to please," McCarthy says.

Dealing with disinterest

Special care needs to be taken when testers appear bored or unimpressed. It can be disheartening to see comments or data that indicate a lack of enthusiasm. Yet this is still an opportunity for the team to ponder what might be causing this reaction. Possibilities include:

- **Small sample size.** One person saying "meh" is not much to go on. However, if a group of testers express similar opinions, that is evidence that something may be wrong with the work.

- **The media is not ready.** This issue can surface with early prototypes. The media may be too incomplete or rough around the edges, and test audiences are simply unable to connect with the experience.

- **The audience is not ready.** This comes up with particularly visionary works that take novel approaches to production, form, or content. The works may be considered ahead of their time, but they are still too unfamiliar for most audiences.

- **Right media, wrong audience.** The team has a fantastic project under development, but the test audience does not respond to the prototypes because it's the wrong group of people.

- **Right audience, wrong media.** The team has a great idea and the right audience lined up to view the prototypes, but they do not respond because of poor execution and/or a lack of intangibles for the audience to connect with.

- **Wrong media, no audience.** The team produces media for which there is no real audience.

Some of the situations described above can be remedied. For instance, if the test audience is too small, more people can be recruited. If the team suspects the wrong audience is being tested, find a new group of people to work with. And if it becomes apparent that the prototype is not enough to elicit useful feedback, a more complete or polished prototype can be shown to testers.

Other situations are not so easily remedied. For a creative team that is ahead of its time, test audiences may not "get it" when they view the first prototypes. Eventually they may come around if society catches up, or the talented team is somehow able to make the test audience appreciate the new forms or special content they are working on. But that is the exception rather than the rule. Most cutting-edge media will never be widely appreciated by audiences, no matter how talented the creators are. And that's perfectly acceptable for media vision-aries. Getting their cutting-edge media out to the world is far more important to them than achieving mainstream success.

As for poorly produced media that fails to move test audiences, the creative team can hopefully learn from the feedback and successfully iterate. If not, it may be necessary to go back to the drawing board.

Finally, there are those rare cases in which there really isn't an audience for the product. Acid Jazz performed on kazoos or a science fiction sitcom starring a family of alien slime creatures is unlikely to connect with anybody, no matter how well the works are produced. Audiences will never love such media, and no amount of iteration will save them. It's either back to the drawing board, or it's time to abandon the idea altogether.

Takeaways

- In Lean Media productions, stakeholder feedback takes a back seat, while audience feedback informs the core team.

- Teams are not necessarily looking for suggestions from test audiences, and are not obliged to act on feedback.

- Some creators will be averse to seeking feedback on a work in progress, because they are perfectionists, don't like criticism, or are sensitive about leaks. However, there are ways to address such concerns.

- It's normal to get conflicting feedback. Try to zero in on themes or specific issues that are cited by multiple testers.

- Disinterest can indicate problems with the intangible qualities of the work. It might also point to sampling issues, a media/audience mismatch, or media that is ahead of its time.

CHAPTER 9

Pivot or abandon

If you follow news about tech startups, you have undoubtedly heard the term "pivot." It's a hot idea in Silicon Valley and other tech hubs, and is closely associated with the Lean Startup movement. In *The Lean Startup*, Eric Ries defines a pivot as a "fundamental change to [a startup's] business strategy" borne out of necessity, such as failing to gain traction and/or making a crucial discovery about customers' needs.

One oft-cited example of pivoting involves Twitter, the popular social network that launched in 2006. Twitter did not start out as a social network. Its origins lie in Odeo, a long-forgotten podcast directory whose founders realized that an internal communications tool for sharing short messages showed more promise than downloadable audio programs. Twitter now has hundreds of millions of devoted users all over the world.

It should be noted that pivots have been part of the technology landscape for many years. One of my favorite examples is Nintendo, a Japanese company that dominated a large segment of the global video game industry for more than three decades. It started out as a manufacturer of Japanese playing cards in the late 1800s, pivoted into toys and food in the 1960s, and pivoted once again into video games in the late 1970s. It is now known for iconic games and gaming platforms, including *Donkey Kong*, *Super Mario Bros.*, *Pokémon*, and the NES, Nintendo Wii and Nintendo Switch gaming consoles.

While pivots are hugely popular, the term can be misused. Silicon Valley firms sometimes spin unwelcome news by blaming a "pivot" for poor performance, layoffs, or some other problem. Other firms might hype a new feature or rebranding as a pivot, when in reality little has changed. The term has also wormed its way into politics, to describe a change in a candidate's policy or strategy.

For media, pivoting encompasses everything from a major shift in work under development, to a complete reset. An author tearing up a poorly received manuscript and starting over from scratch is a pivot. So is a situation in which a film studio dumps the director and brings in a new writer to overhaul the script. A news magazine that rebrands itself and switches to an all-online video format represents a pivot, as it will require shaking up the creative team and developing a new online audience.

However, pivoting does not refer to new elements, higher production values, or some other improvement being applied to a work in progress. When a musician takes a demo version of a new song and re-records it in a professional studio, that is not a pivot. Nor is a book moving from the idea stage to a rough draft, or a new video game entering the soft-launch phase after three months of prototyping and user testing. In the Lean Media context, these types of improvements are part of the iterative development process. A pivot is more substantive, and implies moving in a new direction as opposed to improving or developing an existing work.

Chubby pivots

Media pivots are rarely discussed in public. Unlike in Silicon Valley, where failure is celebrated and successful pivots are the stuff of legend, pivots involving traditional media brands or big-budget projects are regarded as proof that something (or someone) isn't working out. When pivots do occur, many media companies will use different language to emphasize the change in direction and/or the new team—a "reboot" or "rebranding" to focus on some special opportunity.

For instance, in 2015 the well-established (and apparently profitable) magazine *Organic Gardening* pivoted to a new focus, a new audience, and a new name—*Organic Life*. The goal of the rebranding was to emphasize the whole organic lifestyle, as opposed to just organic gardening. A new editor was brought on board to lead the charge. The pivot was a logical step in the magazine's evolution, as opposed to some aspect of the magazine having failed.

For unreleased works in progress, however, it is harder to portray a pivot as an evolutionary step. One famous example involved *The Wizard of Oz*. The 1939 fantasy is now regarded as a classic, but production was a disaster. It was a complicated, expensive film that encountered all kinds of difficulties, ranging from actors falling ill to issues with new color film cameras. After seeing the rough cuts, the producer decided to replace the director as well. A new creative advisor (director George Cukor) insisted that costumes and other elements had to be redone, while a new director (Victor Fleming) was brought in to completely reshoot the film. However, Fleming and Cukor were unable to complete *The Wizard of Oz* after being called in to rescue *Gone with the Wind* (which was experiencing production difficulties itself). So, a third director was brought in to wrap up shooting for *Oz!*

The public knew almost nothing about the pivot and the behind-the-scenes drama, though. Audiences loved the movie, and eight decades later *The Wizard of Oz* is still regarded as a classic and one of the greatest Hollywood success stories.

Not all pivots for in-progress works end up being so successful. *Chinese Democracy*, the sixth studio album by the hard-rock band Guns 'n' Roses, went through a grinding pivot over a period of many years. Various band members and producers cycled through the project as lead singer Axl Rose changed his mind about the songs and the sound he wanted. Although an album's worth of songs was recorded in the late 1990s, they were scrapped, reworked, and rerecorded a few years later. The completed album was finally released in late 2008 after running up more than $13 million in production costs. While *Chinese Democracy* was certified platinum within a few months, sales quickly dropped off. One retailer was stuck with excess inventory of the album, which it was forced to remainder for just $2 per disc. Today, few Guns 'n' Roses fans regard *Chinese Democracy* as the band's best effort, and the band rarely plays the songs live.

Lean Media pivots

The *Wizard of Oz* and *Chinese Democracy* were expensive projects that used the chubby approach to developing media, with lots of planning, secrecy, and launch hype. The projects pivoted because of internal issues, ranging from evolving creative visions to personality clashes. *Organic Gardening* pivoted decades after launching, in response to changing market conditions and a new vision for the brand. In all three examples, there were significant shifts in the ways the works were produced, as well as in the makeup of the creative teams.

In a Lean Media setting, a pivot is far more likely to take place in response to issues relating to a new understanding of the audience, as opposed to internal problems or creative differences. There may not be any changes in personnel, although radical pivots may require new members with different skill sets.

At the end of the last chapter, I outlined several situations that can trigger a Lean Media pivot. They include works that have trouble connecting with test audiences, which could be caused by missing intangibles or targeting the wrong audience. As a creator, it can be disheartening to realize that almost no one likes your baby, even after repeated iterations and quality improvements. While it may be tempting to keep plugging away, consistent negative feedback and disinterest are signs that it is time to shift direction.

A Lean Media pivot can happen at any stage, from the time the idea is conceived to after the flex launch. The earlier the pivot takes place, the fewer resources will be wasted on a project that is probably destined to fail.

On the other hand, if it's too early the creative team may not have a fully formed idea of the media experience. There may also be insufficient audience feedback to work with. Team members may assume that the media will not resonate with audiences, but if only a few testers have been involved thus far, there's a real risk they are not getting the full picture.

At the other end of the spectrum, waiting until much later in the development process allows the team to make a more informed decision based on lots of feedback gathered over the course of multiple iterations. There are three significant drawbacks to waiting so long to pivot, though:

1. Should the team decide to pivot so late in the game, a lot of time, effort, and money will have already been wasted.

2. If the pivot takes place after a flex launch, there may have to be some sort of official public statement about the change.

3. If there is a situation in which some audience members liked the original media but most did not, the team may also have to deal with vocal complaints from the disappointed minority.

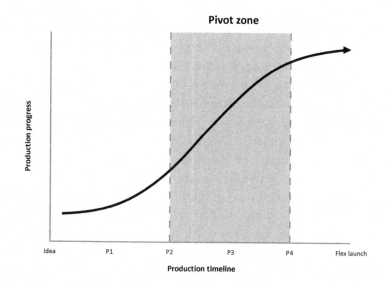

For these reasons, I recommend that pivots take place during the middle or late prototyping stage (see diagram). By this point, not only will the work be beyond the ideation stage and the first rough prototypes, but there also should be a solid feedback history that the team can use to make better-informed decisions. While some prototypes may already be public, audiences (and media critics) will generally be more forgiving if the media is clearly in the midst of development as opposed to the flex launch version, which will already be quite polished.

Feedback has an essential role to play both before and after the pivot. Assuming audience-related issues were behind the pivot, it will be necessary for audiences to re-evaluate the project once the team has branched off into a new direction. Depending on whether the same audience is being targeted, or a different group of people needs to be exposed, the team (or the marketing group) needs to set up testing scenarios to gather more feedback.

Ideally, the early remakes will generate feedback that indicates the pivot was the right move to make. However, the team may also encounter problems with the pivoted version. It may be necessary to pivot again—or abandon the project altogether.

Pivoting from one format to another

An excellent example of a Lean Media pivot is the 1999 movie *Office Space*. The low-budget comedy, directed by Mike Judge, follows a group of frustrated coworkers in a suburban office park. It barely eked out a profit during its theatrical release. Yet the script, the acting, the hip-hop soundtrack, and various intangible elements (such as the odd role played by a red stapler) came together in a way that was irresistible to young audiences. The film soon gained cult status, and had a strong second life in DVD and cable reruns.

Office Space did not start out as a film. It was basically a pivot from an earlier work by Judge; a series of animated shorts called *Milton*, about a hapless office worker dominated by his boss. There were only a handful of episodes, which aired in the early 1990s on Comedy Central, MTV, and *Saturday Night Live*. Much like the early *Simpsons* bumpers, *Milton* clips were just 1 to 2 minutes long and crudely put together—Judge, who had studied physics in college, was a self-taught animator and voiced Milton and the other characters in the office. The indie cartoon was mildly popular but hardly memorable, and the series went on hiatus as Judge moved on to more promising projects, including *Beavis and Butthead* and *King of the Hill*.

If *Milton* couldn't make it on its own as an animated series, perhaps there was another opportunity on the big screen. Mainstream viewers did not particularly care about the quirky office worker and his boss when they were presented in 90-second-long bursts. But when it came to *Beavis and Butthead* and *King of the Hill*, audiences really connected with Judge's longer scripts, fully-formed characters, and offbeat humor.

Judge got the backing of Twentieth Century Fox to expand *Milton* into a full-length movie script, including a half-dozen new characters. They also let him direct *Office Space* even though he had never worked on a live-action film before.

The pivot came late, but it worked. Focus groups loved the soundtrack. While the film barely broke even at theaters, millions of DVD and VHS copies were sold, and it did well on cable television, too. The film also helped launch Judge's film and live-action television career (more recently he is the creator of HBO's hit series, *Silicon Valley*).

Pivoting to new audiences

Early in my own career, I was involved in a new media project that would have been a perfect pivot. In the mid-1990s, a Taiwanese broadcaster hired me to help produce a daily English-language television newscast. Why have an English TV show in a market that had more than 20 million Mandarin and Taiwanese speakers, but only a small population of foreigners residing in the country? This was the thinking behind the program:

- Taiwan's political leadership (which controlled the island's three terrestrial broadcast networks) wanted to transform Taiwan into an international business hub to better compete with Hong Kong, Singapore, and China. A strong English-language media would help improve Taiwan's international image.

- The broadcaster believed there was a large enough expatriate audience to attract advertisers.

- Until advertising or some other funding source came online, the broadcaster was willing to subsidize the experiment.

The network did not have a Lean Media outlook. Largely sheltered from competition (cable television had only recently appeared in Taiwan) the network had become bureaucratic and conservative in its approach to making television programs.

No one cared about reducing waste. In fact, the broadcaster was willing to devote all kinds of resources to the English newscast. It reassigned several reporters, camera operators, and editors from Chinese programs to work on the English newscast, and hired two anchors, three translators, and a producer/narrator/scriptwriter (me).

The executive producer made plans for a show that followed a standard television news format. We were given an early morning weekday slot to broadcast the program live. We had a few weeks to get some processes in place and do a few dry runs, and then we launched. As part of the chubby launch marketing, there was some local press coverage and other promotions. But the program itself was never shown to test audiences before the launch date. The only feedback was internal.

After the launch, we didn't really know what our target audience thought of the program, because ratings weren't available for a few months. When we asked our expatriate friends for their opinions, more often than not the response was, "I couldn't get up at 6:30 in the morning to watch it."

When the ratings finally did come in, it was clearly a disaster. Few people were watching the program—the ratings for the program were just a few tenths of a percentage point. It was not just a failure to connect with audiences, it also represented a business failure—a lack of eyeballs meant few advertisers were interested.

The team tweaked some elements of the newscast in an attempt to make it more appealing, including covering stories that we thought were more likely to interest expatriate audiences. Later, the audience grew thanks to distribution on a local airline's in-flight entertainment system. We also determined that a lot of English language learners were tuning in. But it wasn't enough to right the ship. Station management quickly lost interest in the newscast. We were shifted to an even earlier slot, and started losing reporters and other resources to the Mandarin newscast that started later in the morning. Two years after the English newscast launched, the broadcaster pulled the plug.

At the time the cancellation was announced, I believed the failure could be attributed to the fact that there wasn't a big enough audience in Taiwan for a daily English newscast. But two decades later, through the lens of Lean Media, I now regard the failure in a different light.

Part of the problem related to our chubby mindset. Forget prototyping or audience surveys. We created a professionally produced and expensive program, based on a format that seemed safe to network executives and stakeholders seated around a conference room table. We had little understanding of our target audience, and did not attempt to run focus groups or gather feedback, which could have identified problems or helped with program development.

Moreover, once the newscast launched, we largely ignored the limited feedback that we did receive, such as the complaint that the program was too early or most of our audience consisted of local people who wanted to study English.

Even if we had taken a lean approach to developing the program, it wouldn't have guaranteed success. However, doing so would have potentially headed off an expensive experiment, and perhaps even led to an interesting pivot focused more on the needs of our secondary audience—English language learners.

Had we acted, it would have been an intriguing outcome. We weren't even trying to attract native Mandarin and Taiwanese speakers; they just tuned in to the newscast because it was an opportunity to hear fluent English speakers (the anchors, reporters, and narrators) talking in English about topics that were familiar to them.

What would the pivot have looked like? Here are some of things we could have tested:

- Adding English subtitles based on the scripts and teleprompter text.

- Creating a Mandarin segment at the beginning and/or the end of each newscast to discuss English vocabulary, grammar, and other English usage issues relating to the day's broadcast.

- Working with a local publishing company to create a magazine, book, or newspaper supplement for local residents interested in using the TV newscast as the basis for improving vocabulary and listening comprehension.

These ideas may sound like a stretch. But what else could we do? Our original target audience was small, numbering between 50,000 and 100,000 native English speakers and Western expats. By and large they were not keen in getting up at daybreak to watch the newscast. Rescheduling to later in the day was out of the question—it would have threatened the network's cash cows, Mandarin and Taiwanese programming watched by millions of people every day. A pivot was the only alternative to failure, and the network chose to shut it down.

Would a program targeting English language learners have worked? I believe so, based on the success of another program that did something similar. Around the same time the newscast was winding down, a local publishing company created a successful franchise that established a daily English language television tutorial (complete with skits featuring native speakers) and a companion magazine. It eventually grew to hundreds of thousands of subscribers and monthly newsstand sales. One of my colleagues from the English newscast ended up working there, and enjoyed a lengthy career helping local people improve their

English. To network television executives and Taiwan's political leaders, an English tutorial may not be as sexy as a news program, but it has arguably done more to help Taiwan's international business stature by helping hundreds of thousands of local people speak better English.

For struggling creative teams using the Lean Media framework, pivoting may not be an option. Or, even if it is an option, the pivot itself may fail. If that's the case, it may be time to let the project go and move on to something else.

Abandoning a project

In Silicon Valley, failure is a fetish. Founders, venture capitalists, and pundits relentlessly promote the idea that learning from failure is one of the best ways to improve products, find customers, and build a successful business. Unlike in other cultures that regard failure as a mark of shame, in Silicon Valley, failure is seen as a badge of honor.

Paradoxically, few in Silicon Valley or other U.S. startup centers like to talk about abandoning a project. If a business idea or a new product fails in the marketplace, the idea is to keep pivoting until you have exhausted your funds ("out of runway," in startup parlance) or it is otherwise no longer possible to keep going. Only then it is acceptable to embrace failure. The entrepreneur who never gives up is the ideal; people who fold too early are either weak or were never really cut out for entrepreneurship in the first place, or so the thinking goes.

I have some experience with tech startups. In the early teens, I co-founded a mobile software company. It lasted about a year before we pulled the plug. It could have kept going for at least another six months on the seed capital I had raised. However, after my cofounder announced he was leaving and we encountered a major business obstacle, it did not seem possible to continue the venture or pivot the business into something else.

One Boston-area startup advisor, after hearing me explain why I was winding down the venture and returning most of the seed capital to investors, was surprised. In his view, a failing startup with a little bit of runway still had lots of options, including:

- Fixing the problem(s)

- Raising more money

- Selling the company and its assets

- Pivoting

Shutting down the company with money in the bank was not on his list of possible outcomes. However, the advisor acknowledged that many startups in a similar situation often found themselves falling into two unattractive operating modes:

1. Putting on a "fake it 'til you make it" mask, and pretend that everything is going great until it (hopefully) succeeds.

2. Joining the ranks of the "walking dead"—startups that have no real hope of achieving success, but still have enough investor capital to keep operating.

In the media world, I believe a different outlook is warranted. Sure, failure is a fantastic teacher. But is it really necessary to keep plugging away at a publication, video series, gaming app, or musical production that is unable to connect with an audience or balance its creative goals with business realities?

In my opinion, if the media you are working on has no realistic hope of finding an audience, and a pivot either doesn't work or is unfeasible, it's time to abandon the project and move on. There is no need to fake it until you make it, shuffle the creative or business teams, or spend loads of money and time trying to fix problems that are probably unfixable. If it looks hopeless—and you will probably know when it has reached that point—just put down your pen, or your keyboard, or your camera, and walk away.

Abandoning a project should be relatively straightforward if you are a solo creator such as a musician, game designer, or author. The shutdown will probably involve archiving some computer files before going on to the next project.

This is what I did when my first attempt at writing a novel turned into a failure. I have always wanted to write a novel, and in 2014 I took part in National November Writing Month (NaNoWriMo) to produce a rough draft of a science fiction story. I had been thinking about writing a novel for a few years, and had a few ideas percolating in my head. The plot was somewhere between Arthur C. Clarke's *Rendezvous with Rama* and a classic Chinese adventure story, with a rich slate of characters and lots of action to keep the narrative moving along. It did not take long to bang out a rough draft.

Beta readers had a tepid reaction to the draft. I posted chapters on Wattpad, but no one cared. I wrote a series of short stories based on the same fantasy world, but they were rejected by every science fiction magazine I approached. People simply weren't interested in the world, its characters, or my way of telling the stories. My options were spending many months rewriting the novel, or abandoning the idea. I chose to bail. It wasn't hard to do; I simply stopped working on the novel and archived the manuscript and short stories on Dropbox.

If you are on a creative team with many members, are working for a large media company, or have a big existing audience, things can get complicated. Once the train leaves the station, it may be difficult to stop. You may know it's time to abandon a project that's going nowhere, but your team members may insist on continuing. There may also be disagreements with colleagues working on the business side of the house about whether or not to shut down a project. Even if early feedback and other indicators are telling you the project won't fly, others may be so invested in the creative vision or the business possibilities that they cannot accept prematurely shutting it down. Hardcore fans may also be disappointed to learn that a production by their favorite creative team has been scuttled.

There is no easy way to get around these types of disagreements, although it helps if there is another promising project queued up and ready to move forward. Regardless, when you do pull the plug or walk away, try to avoid burning bridges with your team, creative or business partners, or audiences. You may need them (and they may need you!) in the future.

Lastly, when walking away from a project, there is no need to feel shame. It's not like an utterly lopsided basketball game in which the losing team is locked into the competition and forfeiting is not an option. Failing media projects can be abandoned. Every media person knows what it's like to work on something that flops, and most would agree that it's better to get out early, before it turns into an expensive flop.

Audiences, too, are familiar with horrible albums and movies, uninspiring games, boring websites, and other bad media. They won't blame you for making the decision to kill off something that's not worth their time or attention.

Onto the next project

The learning experiences from failure are real. Think back to the last time you worked on media that crashed and burned in front of audiences, or had to be prematurely abandoned. Sure, it was a horrible experience, but perhaps you were able to try a new process or technology that gave you a leg up on your next project. Or, you learned that a certain audience is not worth targeting.

Negative experiences can also steer creators in different directions in the future, or can increase the chances of success the next time around because they will know what not to do.

In certain cases, failure can lead directly to spectacular success. It's positively exhilarating when a failed film, recording session, or digital creation leads to an incredible collaboration or groundbreaking ideas.

There is a long history of failed boy bands and girl groups that have resulted in spectacular solo singing careers after the singer has a chance to work with a certain musician, songwriter, or producer. Michael Jackson's post-Jackson 5 solo career was launched after working with composer Quincy Jones on the box-office flop *The Wiz*. Producer L.A. Reid signed the girl group Choice to his label in the 1990s. The group went nowhere, but he later worked with one of the singers, Pink, on a series of pop albums that rocketed to the top of the charts.

Strategic abandonment

It's possible to run several pivot-or-abandon projects simultaneously. This may seem counterintuitive—if you are participating in several development projects at once, members will be unable to focus their creativity on any one work, or may be distracted by whichever project happens to be struggling the most. But this approach allows teams to spread out the risk and transfer ideas between projects. Through this process, the team can gradually whittle away the losers and concentrate on the most promising works.

Here's an example. In the mid-2000s, when I was working for tech news publisher IDG, I helped create an experimental tech news aggregator called *Tech Dispenser*. The idea: Present a never-ending list of interesting tech headlines from across the web for users to click on, kind of like *The Drudge Report* or Google News, and let participating tech sites carry IDG-sourced advertising via a special widget.

It was a lean operation, with just a small creative team consisting of myself, a project/business manager, a developer, and a graphic designer. We also had support from the company's general manager who provided the funding and mandate for us to push the project forward.

Late in the prototyping stage, it became clear that *Tech Dispenser* was failing. We used newsletters and promotions from our other websites to drive traffic to techdispenser.com, and set up a Twitter feed. However, visitors rarely came back for more headlines. Even after making some tweaks to the content and interface, the traffic was negligible. There were also workflow issues related to the content management system.

The Tech Dispenser Twitter feed. The news service never had a large audience, but the concept of a distributed advertising network turned into a huge money-maker for IDG.

The GM made the call to pull the plug on the editorial site. Everyone on the team knew the site was unlikely to go anywhere, so there were no hard feelings when the *Tech Dispenser* website was retired. The service pivoted to a custom newsletter, which wound down a few years later. However, the monetization plan for *Tech Dispenser* evolved to become the IDG Tech Network, a highly successful advertising network and revenue generator that delivers more than one billion impressions per month across the globe.

When the editorial arm of *Tech Dispenser* was amputated, that was not the end of our jobs. All of us had other responsibilities at IDG. Indeed, all of us were involved with other online and mobile experimentation taking place across the organization. Once *Tech Dispenser* was no longer active, we had more cycles to devote to other special projects. Some of the remaining development projects would also be shut down, but there were a few that ended up succeeding. One of them—a specialty blog called *IT Blogwatch*—lasted more than 10 years.

Importantly, running multiple development projects at once allowed us to transfer successful ideas between projects, even if the projects themselves were failing. For instance, an online community called *Shark Bait* used the same content management system that had proved to be so effective for our blogging presence. *Shark Bait* also borrowed the headline-centric approach we had first tried out with *Tech Dispenser*, and generated 4 million page views in its first year.

Takeaways

- A startup pivot represents a shift in business strategy. A Lean Media pivot represents a major shift in the content, often based on a new understanding of audiences.

- Pivots taking place during the mid-to-late prototyping stages are ideal, as there should be lots of feedback and a better idea of what elements are problematic.

- It will be necessary for audiences to re-evaluate the project once the project has pivoted. If the audience itself has changed, new testers will need to be recruited.

- If iteration and pivots fail, it is time to abandon the work and move onto something else.

- Try to avoid burning bridges with other team members, stakeholders, and fans. Leave the door open for something even better to rise out of the ashes.

10

The Lean Media project planner

By now you've read about Lean Media concepts, and have learned how creative teams have leveraged them to reduce risk and create great media. It's time to put these ideas to work for your own creations, using the Lean Media project planner. The project planner is a one-page template that creators can use to plan the iterative development of new works, from idea to launch.

For readers who have worked in tech startups, the project planner may seem similar to the "business model canvas" template used by mainstream businesses, which was later adopted for the Lean Startup framework. However, unlike these business-oriented canvases, the Lean Media project planner is focused solely on product development, and does not attempt to track cost structure, revenue streams, or other business metrics.

Moreover, the project planner doesn't just segment the project into distinct stages. It also emphasizes the different teams that will be working on each stage of development, and records notes about target audiences and test audiences. As you know from reading Chapter 7, understanding your audiences is a key part of the Lean Media framework, so audiences naturally figure prominently in such planning.

Anyone associated with the creation of a media project can use the project planner. Most will probably be creators or members of the production team.

For corporate-driven projects, people from the business side of the house will likely participate. If you are working with a business group, take the opportunity to make planning for the project a collaborative effort. This will get everyone on the same page regarding the project's progression as well as other crucial elements such as determining the target audience(s) and team makeup as the project evolves. However, in line with the Lean Media principle of reducing waste, avoid including business stakeholders in creative decision-making or nonessential approvals.

The project planner will be most useful to creators or teams who are formulating an idea, or are still at the early prototyping stages. It can serve as an important roadmap for product development and audience testing going forward. There may also be some opportunities to think about ways of incorporating audience feedback into later iterations. By the time you have passed the flex launch, there is no real point to using the project planner. That is, unless you are considering a pivot . . . or a post mortem.

How to fill out the project planner

Here's what the planner looks like (you can also download blank templates from leanmedia.org):

Project Name/Description	Target Audience(s)		
	Prototype 1	Prototype 2	Prototype 3	Prototype 4/Flex launch
Team				
Product				
Audience/ feedback				

In the top left corner is a description of the project or the idea. If you have a working title, put it here, followed by a sentence or two describing other relevant aspects or elements.

The box in the upper right section of the page will contain a description of your audience(s). Be sure to include a few bullets describing your target or ideal audience. Keep in mind that you may need to update this section as you learn more about your audience through various feedback channels.

The document assumes most media projects involve multiple prototypes, starting with wireframes/sketches/mockups, working up to demo versions and functioning models, and finally reaching a fairly polished state. For some types of media, such as a feature film or video game, there may be far more than three or four iterative stages between ideation and launch. However, the idea here is not to precisely document the nitty-gritty details of each update. Rather, it's to have a general idea of the main stages of development, and the teams and test audiences that will be associated with each.

Underneath the prototype stages are boxes describing the team. For many projects, it's not just the core creative team (or sole creator) who will be involved with production. Different people (and partners) will be involved at each stage.

For instance, in a Hollywood movie production, the people involved at the beginning of the production (screenwriter, producer, studio planners) will only have a limited overlap with the team taking the lead in the middle stages (director, actors, set builders, lighting and sound professionals). In the late stages of production, many of those involved in the live shoot will move on, as editors, sound engineers, and CGI experts take over.

For a big project, there won't be enough space on the project planner to include everyone's name, so just include departments or key players. Remember, reducing waste is one of the foundation principles of Lean Media, so teams should be lean—ideally, a team should only include enough people necessary to carry the production forward, with little or no skills/talent overlap.

The next row is for product notes. Again, this is not the spot to write out the nitty-gritty details. This is a place to broadly describe what's going on at each stage in the production, or to list milestones. As we will see in our examples below, some of the points listed here will tie into audience feedback mechanisms from earlier stages.

The audience/feedback box is larger than the product and team boxes. This is no accident. It is here that you will identify the test audiences and mechanisms by which to gather feedback from them. The test audiences can be detailed—at the earliest prototype stages, you may even list individuals' names, depending on what sort of media you are working on (e.g., "Beta readers Tamara, Arthur, and Liz"). Later, as you expose the prototypes to bigger test audiences, the description will become more general—"30 members of the fan club" or "Portland and Los Angeles focus groups."

As for feedback mechanisms, jot down how you will survey your test audiences and bring the qualitative comments and quantitative data such as survey responses and tracking reports back to the team. For instance, if you are allowing a few select members of your fan club to listen to some home demos, you might write "Feedback session led by Carmen, David taking notes." If it is a mobile news service, you may turn to in-app analytics software to provide quantitative information.

Keep in mind that the project planner does not need to be completely filled out in one go. This is especially true at the ideation stage or the first prototype. You and your team may only have a limited sense of how the production will progress, or may not know what kinds of test audiences to recruit or how to gather feedback from them. It's OK to leave some columns blank, or scrawl TBD (to be determined) in the audience/feedback field until you have a better idea of how to proceed. Should the team decide to pivot, you may need to start all over again with a blank template.

One thing you will not find in the project planner is dates. There are several reasons for this. The Lean Media project planner is not a detailed tracking document, but rather a tool that can help outline the project, teams, and audiences. In addition, at the earliest stages of production, planning a timeline may not be clear.

If you do know certain dates, or want to include them, you can pencil them in. But for serious tracking purposes, use a calendar, a spreadsheet, or a professional-grade project planning tool to identify key deadlines and cascading timelines.

A project planner for *Napoleon Dynamite*

At this point, it may be helpful to apply the Lean Media project planner to actual media. Let's start with a high-profile example from the world of independent filmmaking: *Napoleon Dynamite*.

The film has the hallmarks of an indie classic. Conceived and created by a group of film students at Brigham Young University, *Napoleon Dynamite* stars Jon Heder as a high-strung teenaged nerd living in a rural community and overcoming various challenges related to family, school, and small-town life. Shot on a budget of just $400,000, it was a breakout hit at the 2004 Sundance Film Festival and quickly became a cult phenomenon, grossing nearly $45 million within a year.

The production history of *Napoleon Dynamite* reveals a Lean Media narrative. There was a strong creative core consisting of husband and wife screenwriters

Jared and Jerusha Hess as well as their BYU classmate Jon Heder, prototypes including multiple scripts and a nine-minute black-and-white student film *Peluca*, feedback cycles from student competitions and film festivals, and a soft launch at Sundance. Here's how the team might have approached the project if they had a copy of the Lean Media project planner in the early 2000s:

Project Name/Description	Target Audience(s)		
Indie feature film about an oddball youth navigating family dynamics, high school friendships, and small town life.	• Students • Film festival audiences • Mainstream audiences?		

	Prototype 1	Prototype 2	Prototype 3	Prototype 4/Flex launch
Team	Core: Jared & Jerusha Hess (writers), Jon Heder (lead actor)	Same core team, Jared directing, plus crew, actors & extras from Preston, Idaho	Core team, producer Jeremy Coon, actor Aaron Ruell (Kip)	Core team, crew (BYU) and cast (mostly Hollywood), local extras
Product	Script for short film *Peluca* developed by students in BYU film program	9-minute black and white film *Peluca*: "A day in the life of Seth, super nerd extraordinaire"	Script for *Napoleon Dynamite*, based on Heder's character	92-minute feature film, *Napoleon Dynamite*
Audience/ feedback	• Internal team feedback based on script readings • Classmates • Film school faculty	• Internal team feedback • Audiences from BYU student film competition • Audience at "Slamdance Film Festival"	• Internal team feedback • Hollywood casting directors • Professional actors	• Internal feedback • Feedback from local extras • Sundance Film Festival program staff • Sundance audiences • Salt Lake City screening

I have filled in the planner based on documented facts such as the key players on the core creative team, the history of the black-and-white short film *Peluca*, and the development of the feature film. However, I have taken a few liberties in describing how the team used audience feedback to improve the screenplays. While the Hesses and Heder paid close attention to audiences during the student screenings and film festivals, they did not actively plan how the feedback would be brought back into the project. It was more a matter of observing the reaction of audiences, validating key elements such as Heder's performance, and expanding the student short film into a full-length feature.

There were several other interesting aspects of how the team used feedback. First, while sold-out screenings and the near-universal positive reactions could be regarded as quantitative indicators, much of the early feedback was qualitative. Second, not all feedback was acted upon, including comments from external stakeholders. This gets back to Chapter 4, which noted that creators should feel empowered to trust their own instincts, and Chapter 6, which discussed the potential for nonessential stakeholders to get in the way.

Taking a look at the project planner, in the name/description box a simple placeholder describes the project—an indie film about a nerdy teenager growing up in a small town. Moving onto the target audiences, the Hesses at first regarded the project as little more than a film school assignment that might get some traction at independent film festivals. Later, the team saw the potential for the film to connect with mainstream audiences.

The first prototype was the script for *Peluca*. Jared and Jerusha Hess worked on the script and asked Heder to play a small role as a bully, but later changed him to the lead role, playing the awkward, nerdy "Seth." Feedback at this stage consisted of Heder reading his parts with the Hesses, and improvising some of the dialogue—iterating the script—based on his own coming-of-age experiences. As a film school project, it's also likely that the script was shown to fellow students at BYU. Later most of the crew recruited for *Peluca* and *Napoleon Dynamite* were students or recent graduates of BYU.

For the second stage of production, the Hesses, Heder, and the small cast and crew relocated to Preston, Idaho (Jared Hess' hometown) to shoot *Peluca*. The team convinced locals to play certain roles and to serve as extras. Made with a budget of just $500, the film is basic, featuring a limited number of shots in the countryside, on a school bus, at the local high school, and inside a thrift shop. It was a low-budget production, but Heder's strong performance stands out.

Indeed, audience feedback revealed that Heder's character was the key element of the story. A student screening in a 1,000-seat theater on the BYU campus in March 2002 sold out based on word-of-mouth reviews. Later, at the indie Slamdance Film Festival, *Peluca* took on a life of its own, and validated the idea that Heder's unusual character could be turned into something bigger. A fellow BYU student, Jeremy Coon, loved what he saw and offered to produce a full-length version of the film. His role was concentrated on the business side, and through his efforts the creative team was able to secure financing for a bigger effort.

The Hesses went back to work on a full-length script (Prototype #3) based on the Seth character renamed "Napoleon." They had already started work on the *Napoleon* script before *Peluca* was shot—Jared Hess said that *Peluca* was a way to "bring this character to life." In addition to Coon, another BYU affiliate joined the production—actor Aaron Ruell, who would play Napoleon's brother Kip.

During the scriptwriting process, feedback was internal, with only the core team and a few other people associated with the production reading draft copies and giving feedback. While audience members were not exposed to the final *Napoleon* script, there was an opportunity to get feedback from external stakeholders once the team turned to professional talent to round out the cast.

Copies of the short film and the draft script were distributed to Hollywood casting directors. Some saw the humor in the script, but other feedback from this group was negative—the professionals thought the story was too weird or they didn't like Heder's character, with some even recommending that Napoleon be recast. Fortunately, the creative team trusted their instincts and stuck with Heder. In addition, some of the professional actors who read the script liked it a lot, and signed on to the project. They included experienced television actors Jon Gries, Haylie Duff, Tina Majorino, Efren Ramirez, and Shondrella Avery.

The final stage on the project planner is the production of the actual film. The team went back to Idaho for the shoot, which took just over three weeks to complete. Jared Hess was the director. It went smoothly. By this point, the team was comfortable with the characters and story, and knew the type of film it wanted to make. There was little improvisation.

Some of the earliest feedback came from the high school students who played extras in *Napoleon Dynamite*. Jared Hess observed them during one of the breaks quoting quirky one-liners from script. This helped him realize that mainstream audiences might also appreciate the film.

But it was the early reactions to the soft launch of the film that finally convinced the team they had made something important. Jared Hess wanted to send a fully edited and scored version of the film to Sundance Film Festival, which would mean delays until the following year. However, producer Jeremy Coon went behind his back and sent a rough cut to the festival organizers.

Hess was angry, but not for long. The Sundance programming staff loved it, and they arranged for the first theatrical version to be shown in one of the larger venues at the 2004 festival. The response was overwhelmingly positive, with laughing and cheering throughout the screening. An early screening to a non-festival audience in Salt Lake City also went over well.

Napoleon Dynamite was picked up for nationwide distribution, and edited slightly before hitting theaters across the country for the hard launch. It proved to be one of the most successful independent films of 2004.

Using the project planner for video development

Napoleon Dynamite was a hit, grossing tens of millions of dollars during its theatrical run. Now let's take a look at how a smaller team can use the Lean Media project planner. Below is a copy of the project planner for a video initiative that I launched at my own company. I created it in February 2016, to flesh out plans for advancing the product and gathering feedback. Here's what I included:

Project Name/Description	Target Audience(s)		
IN 30 MINUTES video (i30 Media)	• English-speaking viewers who want to see mildly complex technologies demonstrated to them • People looking for branded content which has more dependable quality • Budget: Free to $30		

	Prototype 1	Prototype 2	Prototype 3	Prototype 4/Soft launch
Team	Ian (2012-2013)	Ian + designer (2014-2015)	Ian + Udemy staff (Feb 2016)	Ian (March-April 2016)
Product notes	• Quicktime Screencasts based on Twitter, Google Drive, Excel, etc. • Posted to YouTube • Embedded on Website	• More YT videos, esp. conversion topics • Include pro graphics • Reduce talk at beginning based on P1 feedback • Add YT annotations	• Intro to Google Drive & Docs In 30 Minutes (paid course) • Udemy, Gumroad, & other paid options • Udemy standards for lectures, screencasts	• Launch first title - Google Drive & Docs In 30 Minutes video course • Website, newsletter promo, + Udemy promo tools
Audience/ feedback	• Audience viewing stats from YT • YT Audience comments • Website stats (limited) • What do audiences like/dislike?	• Audience viewing data from YouTube. Pay attention to dropoff point • Monitor subscriber totals	• Udemy testers • Other Udemy instructors? • Newsletter subscribers? (use Gumroad codes, add feedback form for qualitative comments)	• Newsletter clickthrough • Udemy data • Add promo video to YouTube?

Unlike most musical recordings, which are launched and never altered, my online video initiative is an ongoing work. The first screencasts were released five years ago, and I am still releasing new videos every month. But whereas I released the earliest clips without much planning, I have since adopted a lean approach that pays close attention to feedback and iterative development.

In my project planner, I have used a general description, as it's intended to cover different types of video. I started with 3- to 5-minute clips that explained how to perform specific tasks ("How to convert a PDF to Google Docs for editing"), but later decided to expand to full-length programs ("Google Drive and Docs In 30 Minutes").

In the target audience box, I was careful to differentiate the group of people I wanted to attract. My audience valued branded, quality video tutorials over low-quality clips posted by random people working out of their bedrooms. Some might even be willing to pay for the videos. I described my audience as "English-speaking" as opposed to "U.S.", which allowed for speakers of English from other parts of the world, including non-native speakers.

At the time I filled out the project planner, I was well beyond the ideation stage and early prototypes. In the first column, I listed the early YouTube videos I had posted about Twitter, Google Drive, and Excel. Audience/feedback consisted of the actual tools I had used to determine what audiences liked and disliked, including YouTube viewing stats and comments from viewers all over the world.

Some of the qualitative feedback from the first prototype—including comments about my preambles being too long—resulted in changes in the next iteration of the product. In addition to quickly getting to the point, the second-generation screencasts included professional graphics and annotations. I also paid more attention to topics that had proved popular during the first prototype stage, such as conversion videos and videos about mobile apps.

For audience feedback during the second stage, I was careful to pay attention to YouTube metrics that showed the drop-off point for viewers. Understanding when viewers stopped watching was essential:

- It could indicate the location of problems in the scripts or on-screen.

- If the drop-off was consistent across all screencasts, it could reflect the point at which viewers were no longer patient enough to continue watching.

- It could serve as a potential location to place calls-to-action or other annotations, before viewers started watching or doing something else.

The graph below shows the drop-off point for one of my more popular videos. Just before the 2-minute mark, audiences start to rapidly drop off. By the end of the clip, fewer than 30% of viewers are still engaged.

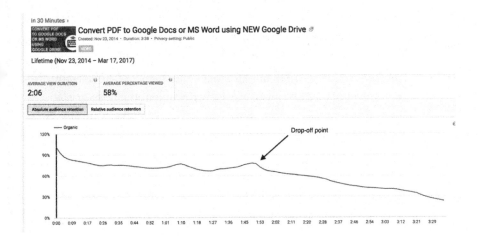

After looking at the data and comparing it against individual videos, I concluded there weren't any technical or content problems with the screencasts. Nor was there some sort of standard patience limit, at which point viewers could no longer stand watching. Rather, most people appeared to drop off at the point at which the main takeaway in each video was communicated. This resulted in more careful positioning of annotations to capture "likes" at the drop-off point, and placing YouTube subscription links and links to my website at the end of each clip.

Prototype 3 and 4 were blank slates at the time I started filling out the project planner. I already knew I wanted to expand into paid, full-length videos on Udemy and elsewhere. This would require higher standards for shooting video and recording audio, as well as following the guidelines issued by the distribution platforms. I also jotted down the audience feedback mechanisms, which would come from the reviews and metrics provided by the respective services. My monthly newsletter would also reveal important data, such as click-through rates on the video promotions relative to the other types of links and articles I included in the newsletter.

Takeaways

- The Lean Media project planner is a tool for creative teams to plan the iterative development of new works, from ideation to flex launch.

- In a media company, creative teams can collaborate with the business side of the house to fill out the Lean Media project planner. This will help get everyone on the same page regarding target audiences, team makeup, and feedback mechanisms.

- If your project has more than four stages, don't worry. The purpose of the project planner is not to precisely document the nitty-gritty details of each update—it's to have a general idea of the main stages of development, and the teams and test audiences that will be associated with each.

- The project planner does not need to be completely filled out in one go. It's OK to leave some columns blank, or scrawl "TBD" in the Audience/feedback field until you have a better idea of how to proceed.

CONCLUSION

The media world is in the midst of tumultuous changes. In the space of a few decades, the ways in which we create media, distribute it, connect with audiences, and generate revenue have been completely altered. Certain types of media have experienced multiple cycles of reinvention.

These are worrying times. Almost as soon as a new technology or process becomes dominant, it is quickly overtaken by an even newer one. Media companies—and the people who create media—once wielded enormous control. Not anymore. Giant tech platforms are the new industry powerbrokers, there is vastly more competition, and business models have squeezed everybody, most notably the people creating and producing media. Many creative people have already left the industry, while others wonder if they can continue their careers.

But these are also exciting times. While technology has brought about disruption, it has also created new opportunities and more efficient ways of getting things done. Few people want to go back to the old days of analog formats or the publisher-dominated business models that limited creative possibilities and the audience experience. The advent of digital media and more open distribution networks have enabled a new generation of creative people to make their marks on the world and bring great media to life.

It's important to keep in mind two immutable constants in the media world:

1. No matter what shiny new app, platform, or process appears on the scene, creative and talented people will still be behind every single great media experience.

2. Audiences will always be looking for something new to interest or inspire them, and will spend their most valuable resource—time—to consume media.

Barring the invention of an artificial intelligence that can completely satisfy our need for works that entertain and inform us, these constants will never change.

What is the role of Lean Media going forward? The framework will not create a new industry order, or overturn well-established ways of developing books, movies, games, websites, music, advertising, and news. However, Lean Media will make a real difference in helping teams understand their audiences and concentrate their creative efforts. For individuals who make media, founders of new media ventures, and professionals working in experienced media teams, the Lean Media framework provides a new perspective that can help creators hone their processes, lower costs, reduce the risk of failure, and ultimately create media that matters.

In the spirit of Lean Media, I am releasing the first edition of this book as a soft launch. I fully expect to revise and iterate in the years following the book's release. Your feedback will be instrumental in improving the framework and providing new insights and examples. Maybe you have implemented Lean Media at your own organization and would like to share your story. Or, perhaps you would like to push back on some of the ideas and examples described in this book. Regardless, I would love to hear from you. On leanmedia.org there are places to leave comments. You can also engage with me on my personal Twitter account (@ilamont), the Lean Media Twitter feed (@leanmediaorg), or the Lean Media Facebook account (facebook.com/leanmediaorg). If you would rather email, send a message to ian@leanmedia.org.

Thanks for reading!

ACKNOWLEDGEMENTS

I have always wondered why book acknowledgements sometimes go on for pages and mention so many people. Now I know! Since 2010, when I first considered how lean concepts might be applied to media works, scores of people have helped shape the Lean Media framework and the manuscript.

More than any other publishing project I have worked on, Lean Media required feedback at practically every stage of development, starting with the idea itself and continuing through multiple drafts, and even the cover and other marketing elements. I was fortunate to have many friends, peers, and audience members who were willing to share their time to help improve the Lean Media framework and book. I also must acknowledge numerous creators from the worlds of film, television, music, gaming, and publishing who inspired me with examples and ideas.

One of the earliest influencers is author and entrepreneur Eric Ries. Had I not attended his Lean Startup talk at MIT in the fall of 2010, this book would not exist. His experience working on IMVU and his thinking around product development inspired me to examine whether Lean Startup concepts could be applied to media creations. While I eventually determined that media requires its own framework and a separate set of methods, basic ideas such as listening to audiences and using iterative development cycles can be traced back to Lean Startup.

Similarly, I must recognize the scholars and Japanese managers who conceptualized the practice of Lean Manufacturing in the 1970s and 1980s. Under this industrial framework, "reducing waste" entailed far more than cutting the fat from budgets. It was an innovative outlook that defined how manufacturers could streamline production and work more efficiently with suppliers. I thought long and hard about how reducing waste might be applied to non-industrial products such as a film or video games. The result can be seen in the Lean Media approaches to building creative teams and working with stakeholders.

Many individuals had a direct impact on the contents of this book. Author, pundit, and friend Jonathan Blum not only listened to my Lean Media pitch, he was also my first beta reader. He gave an honest appraisal and much-needed reality check on various concepts and examples. Jonathan also connected me with editor Zach Gajewski who has done a fine job of helping me structure the book and hone the framework.

Other beta readers included Paul Boutin, Lauren Foster, Monica Hamilton, Jodie Naze, Andrew Kroeger, and Emily Lamont. I deeply value the time they devoted to reading early drafts of the book and sharing their insights.

In recent years, several designers have applied their considerable talents to various publishing projects and Lean Media experiments. The list includes Steve Sauer, Tamara Dever, Rick Soldin, Malgorzata Godziuk, and Monica Thomas, who designed the cover and interior for *Lean Media*.

Professor Cathy Perron, director of the Masters in Media Ventures program at Boston University, was receptive to Lean Media and the book project. Her colleague Jodi Luber helpfully suggested creating a one-page worksheet for creative teams; this eventually became the Lean Media project planner featured in Chapter 10. Serving as a volunteer mentor to some of the graduate students in the Media Ventures program helped me discern the differences between media platforms, media services, and media creators.

I received pushback on some of my early ideas from MIT classmate Juris Barriss, who noted that even non-media companies may want to build products with aesthetic appeal. Bob Hsiung and Andrew Watson pointed out that not every creator wants to make something to please audiences, and may be entirely focused on unique artistic visions. This constructive criticism helped me think through certain aspects of the framework, and make adjustments as development progressed.

A number of media professionals were willing to share their own Lean Media experiences. They include Don Daglow, Bede McCarthy, and N.E.O. Bernhardsson, whose observations were included in the book.

Back when I was running a small software company, entrepreneur Adam Berrey mentored me and showed that not all startups should follow the Minimum Viable Product mantra. His belief in what he calls the "Minimum Delightful Product" helped me think about how test audiences could be shown more polished prototypes of media works during the development phase.

Some years ago, when I first entered the book business, I joined the Independent Book Publishers Association to learn more about publishing and to expand my network. Later, as a board member and participant in IBPA programs, I found that IBPA members are not only receptive to Lean Media, but many also have been practitioners with their own publishing projects. Board colleagues Elizabeth Turnbull, Keith Garton, and Mark Wesley shared their Lean Media stories with me on stage and in the pages of this book. IBPA CEO Angela Bole, former Chair Peter Goodman, and current Chair Rob Price have also been supportive.

I would like to give special thanks to fellow IBPA Executive Committee member Brooke Warner. Her inspirational keynote at the 2017 Publishing University in Portland, Oregon convinced me that the self-directed approach to publishing *Lean Media* was the right path to take. As she says in her book *Greenlight Your Book*, readers are the new gatekeepers, while traditional publishing often entails years-long delays and poor marketing support. Her call-to-action for authors to take control of the publishing process in order to make great books dovetails with the principles of Lean Media. I am grateful for her insights and support.

Former IDG colleagues Martha Connors and Tom Pimental helped recall our shared experiences working on *Tech Dispenser*, cited in Chapter 9. They, along with Johanna Himes, Kevin Gerich, Ken Gagne, Richi Jennings, and Joyce Carpenter, were also on the teams that created or grew projects such as IT Blogwatch, Shark Bait, and Computerworld blogs, also cited in this book. There were many other innovative IDG collaborators I worked with over the years, including Scot Finnie, Eric Hill, Dawn Petersen, Baldwin Louie, Sharon Machlis, Jason Meserve, Derek Butcher, John Sweeney, Ken Mingis, Dave Ramel, Lucas Mearian, and John Gallant. The late IDG founder and chairman Pat McGovern was not only an inspiration, but also encouraged me to apply to business school, a rare transition for people with editorial backgrounds.

Additional feedback came from Michael Malouf, Amy Bennett, Margaret Lamont, Ray Anderson, Natalia Iragorri, Elizabeth Heichler, Ivan Huang, Frédéric Chambour, Phelim Kine, Hiroshi Ogasawara, Janet Norman, Colin Dailey, Paul Tu, and my old *China News* colleague David Smith. Online audiences as well as audience members attending live events have provided valuable feedback about the framework and examples. Members of the Kboards.com "Writer's Café" even helped determine the cover design for this book!

I have to recognize the many other creative collaborators I have worked with over the years, who not only showed me what it means to be part of a creative team, but also how to innovate and improve. In no particular order, this list includes Jeremy Parker, John Rutledge, Dave Rogers, Justin Arey, Nick Makasis, Mark Roe, Amber Chang, Andy Lee, Peggy Wang, Dave Hess, Timo Chen, Steve Tsai, John Winzenburg, Pauline Mu, Simon Reeve, Anthony Lawrance, Jerome Favre, Gavin Phipps, Alicia Beebe, Marc Lacatell, and Jack Morefield.

Last but not least, I would like to thank my wife Nicole. She has patiently put up with my late nights at the computer for years, as I have gone through grad school, launched two companies, and worked on the Lean Media book project. She understands that this is what I need to do, and supports me in whatever way that she can, and for that I am forever grateful.

ABOUT THE AUTHOR

Ian Lamont is the founder of i30 Media Corporation and the creator of the Lean Media framework. His media career has spanned more than 25 years across three continents, including a stint in the British music industry and a six-year residence in Taipei, where he learned Mandarin and worked for a local TV network and newspaper.

After returning to the Boston area, he shifted into digital media, building websites for Harvard University, developing online services for technology publisher IDG, and serving as managing editor of The Industry Standard blog platform and prediction market. Later, Ian founded two ventures, including a mobile software company and i30 Media, which publishes In 30 Minutes guides (in30minutes.com).

Ian is a graduate of the Boston University College of Communication and MIT's Sloan Fellows Program in Innovation and Global Leadership. He lives in the Boston area with his family.

LEAN
MEDIA

BIBLIOGRAPHY

2015 Year In Books Review. Nielsen.

3D TV is officially dead as Sony and LG stop making sets. (2017, January 23). Retrieved from FierceCable: http://www.fiercecable.com/cable/3d-tv-officially-dead-as-sony-and-lg-stop-making-sets

4 Reasons 2015 Could Be the Movie Industry's Worst Year Ever. (2013, August 6). Retrieved from Cracked.com: http://www.cracked.com/quick-fixes/4-reasons-2015-could-be-movie-industrys-worst-year-ever/

A close up of Zynga. (2014, February 23). Retrieved from Kissmetrics: https://blog.kissmetrics.com/zynga-statistics/

Ackley, S. (2017, May 10). *Retail, General Services and Automotive Businesses are Top Spenders in California.* Retrieved from BIA Kelsey: http://blog.biakelsey.com/index.php/2017/05/10/retail-general-services-and-automotive-businesses-are-top-spenders-in-california/

Adams, S. (2015, September 22). Scott Adams: The Man Behind Dilbert. (T. Ferriss, Interviewer) Tim Ferriss Podcast.

Amy Schumer, Funny Girl. (2013, April 18). *The New York Times.* Retrieved from http://www.nytimes.com/2013/04/21/arts/television/amy-schumers-comedy-central-show-from-the-inside.html

Andreesen, M. (2007). *Product/Market Fit.* Retrieved from https://web.stanford.edu/class/ee204/ProductMarketFit.html

Boutin, P. (2016, December). (I. Lamont, Interviewer)

Bushnell, N. (2017, February 27). How I Built This: Atari & Chuck E. Cheese's Nolan Bushnell.

Buzzfeed's Jonah Peretti goes long. Retrieved from Medium: https://medium.com/matter/buzzfeeds-jonah-peretti-goes-long-e98cf13160e7#.ygsr82ah6

Case, G. (2007). *Jimmy Page: Magus, Musician, Man: An Unauthorized Biography.* Hal Leonard Publishing Corporation.

Chadburn, M., & Lahav, G. (2016). *A faster FT.com.* Retrieved from Engine Room blog: http://engineroom.ft.com/2016/04/04/a-faster-ft-com/

Cormier, R. (2015, October 15). *20 Things You Might Not Know About 'Office Space'.* Retrieved from Mental Floss: http://mentalfloss.com/article/61686/20-things-you-might-not-know-about-office-space

Crowe, C. (1975, March 13). The Durable Led Zeppelin: A conversation with Jimmy Page and Robert Plant. *Rolling Stone*. Retrieved from http://www.rollingstone.com/music/news/the-durable-led-zeppelin-19750313

Daglow, D. (2017, March 15). Email interview with Don Daglow. (I. Lamont, Interviewer)

Davis, J. (2006, June 18). Hip-hop, you don't stop. *The Guardian*. Retrieved from https://www.theguardian.com/music/2006/jun/18/urban

Decker, M. (2004, July 2). Fans, critics flip over film's innocence. *Deseret News*. Retrieved from http://www.deseretnews.com/article/595074408/Fans-critics-flip-over-films-innocence.html

Dolenz, M., & Tork, P. (2016, May 29). The Monkees at 50. (CBS News)

Ferriss, T. (2016, May 18). How to Be Tim Ferriss. Freakonomics Podcast.

For Advertisers: Global Reach. Retrieved 2017, from IDG Tech Network: http://idgtechnetwork.com/for-advertisers/global-reach/

Friedman, J. (2016, July 25). *Definition of author platform*. Retrieved from https://janefriedman.com/author-platform-definition/

Garton, K. (2016, August 12). (I. Lamont, Interviewer) Los Angeles.

Goldberg, D., & Larsson, L. (2013, November 5). The Amazingly Unlikely Story of How Minecraft Was Born. *Wired*. Retrieved from https://www.wired.com/2013/11/minecraft-book/

Goldberg, L. (2016, May 16). *Broadcast TV Scorecard: Complete Guide to What's New, Renewed and Canceled*. Retrieved from Hollywood Reporter: http://www.hollywoodreporter.com/live-feed/broadcast-tv-renewed-canceled-guide-844887

Gucci, F. (2017, February 10). *'Guardians Of the Galaxy Vol. 2' Scores The MCU's First 100 Score From Test Screening*. Retrieved from Movie Pilot: https://moviepilot.com/p/guardians-of-the-galaxy-2-test-screening/4206207

Hollywood Adjusts Netflix Strategy as Cord-Cutting Fears Grow. (2015, September 22). Retrieved from AdAge: http://adage.com/article/media/hollywood-adjusts-netflix-strategy-cord-cutting-fears-grow/300482/

Jenkins, J. (2015, May 11). *A Guest Blog from Stephen King—Yes, that Stephen King*. Retrieved from JerryJenkins.com: http://www.jerryjenkins.com/guest-blog-from-stephen-king/

Jimmy Page interview with Dave Schulps (Trouser Press). (1977, June). Retrieved 2016, from http://www.iem.ac.ru/zeppelin/docs/interviews/page_77.trp

Jimmy Page is Just Wild About Led Zeppelin. (1968, December 27). *Go Magazine*.

Kivel, A. (2015, February 12). Dusting 'Em Off: ShowYouSuck Reflects on MC Hammer's Please Hammer, Don't Hurt 'Em. *Consequence of Sound*. Retrieved from http://consequenceofsound.net/2015/02/showyousuck-reflects-on-mc-hammers-please-hammer-dont-hurt-em/

Knopper, S. (2015, December 3). Books: Behind the Scenes of The Wiz With Michael Jackson. *Time*. Retrieved from http://time.com/4135018/the-wiz-michael-jackson/

Lewis, D., & Pallett, S. (2005). *Led Zeppelin: Concert File*. Omnibus Press.

Mars, B. (2016, November 20). *60 Minutes: Bruno Mars*. CBS News.

Marsh, L. (2015, December 28). The Radical History of 1960s Adult Coloring Books. *The New Republic*. Retrieved from https://newrepublic.com/article/126580/radical-history-1960s-adult-coloring-books

Maurya, A. (2010, August 10). *How to Document Your Business Model On 1 Page*. Retrieved from Lean Stack Blog: https://blog.leanstack.com/how-to-document-your-business-model-on-1-page-a6c91ab73efd#.psk9h53g3

McCalmont, T. (2015, July 8). *15 Metrics All Game Developers Should Know by Heart*. Retrieved from GameAnalytics: http://www.gameanalytics.com/blog/metrics-all-game-developers-should-know.html

McCarthy, B. (2016, June 6). Email interview with Bede McCarthy. (I. Lamont, Interviewer)

Media and entertainment spotlight. (International Trade Administration (ITA), U.S. Department of Commerce) Retrieved from selectusa.gov: https://www.selectusa.gov/media-entertainment-industry-united-states

Meyer, M. (2009, April 10). About that advance. *New York Times*. Retrieved from http://www.nytimes.com/2009/04/12/books/review/Meyer-t.html

Milliot, J. (2016, July 15). Coloring Books For Adults Stay Hot. *Publishers Weekly*. Retrieved from http://www.publishersweekly.com/pw/by-topic/industry-news/bookselling/article/70945-coloring-books-stay-hot.html

Mobile Fact Sheet. (2017). Retrieved from Pew Research Center: http://www.pewinternet.org/fact-sheet/mobile/

Movie Budget and Financial Performance Records. (2017). Retrieved from The Numbers: http://www.the-numbers.com/movie/budgets/

Napoleon Dynamite. Retrieved from IMDB: http://www.imdb.com/title/tt0374900/?ref_=nm_flmg_act_60

Nielsen Music Year-End Report U.S., 2016. The Nielsen Company.

Notes: The Wizard of Oz (1939). (n.d.). Retrieved from Turner Classic Movies: http://www.tcm.com/tcmdb/title/852/The-Wizard-of-Oz/notes.html

Ortved, J. (2007, August). Simpson Family Values. *Vanity Fair*. Retrieved from http://www.vanityfair.com/news/2007/08/simpsons200708

Ortved, J. (2010). *The Simpsons: An Uncensored, Unauthorized History*. Farrar, Straus and Giroux.

Osterwalder, A. *The Business Model Canvas*. Retrieved from Strategyzer: https://strategyzer.com/canvas/business-model-canvas

Peluca. (2003). Retrieved from IMDB: http://www.imdb.com/title/tt0398259/?ref_=nm_flmg_wr_7

Reid, L. (2016, November 7). Music Mogul: L.A. Reid, How I Built This podcast.

Rey, L. V. (1997). *Led Zeppelin Live: An Illustrated Exploration of Underground Tapes*. Hot Wacks Press.

Ries, E. (2010, October 5). Presentation on Lean Startup concepts. Cambridge, Massachusetts.

Ries, E. (2011). *The Lean Startup*. Crown Business.

Ries, E. (2015, April 14). *I Am Eric Ries, Author of the Lean Startup. AMA*. Retrieved from Hacker News: https://news.ycombinator.com/item?id=9370128

Rodale Broadens Its Organic Vision in Rebranded Magazine. (2015, April 12). *New York Times*. Retrieved from https://www.nytimes.com/2015/04/13/business/media/rodale-broadens-its-organic-vision-in-rebranded-magazine.html?_r=0

Satariano, A. (2017, February 15). Angry Birds Maker Rovio May Cut Jobs in Revamp of Functions. *Bloomberg*. Retrieved from https://www.bloomberg.com/news/articles/2017-02-15/angry-birds-maker-rovio-may-cut-up-to-35-jobs-in-revamp-of-units

Shadwick, K. (2005). *Led Zeppelin: The Story of a Band and Their Music, 1968-80*. Backbeat Books.

Shiu, A. (2015, June 24). *Zynga Analytics at its Peak*. Retrieved from Amplitude Blog: https://amplitude.com/blog/2015/06/24/zynga-analytics-at-its-peak/

Songwriters: Spotify doesn't pay off ... unless you're a Taylor Swift. (2014, November 13). Retrieved from CNN.com: http://www.cnn.com/2014/11/12/tech/web/spotify-pay-musicians/

Steinberg, B. (2015, January 28). Is TV Making Up for Lost Viewership by Stuffing More Ads Onscreen? *Variety*. Retrieved from http://variety.com/2015/tv/news/is-tv-making-up-for-lost-viewership-by-stuffing-more-ads-on-screen-1201417470/

Television Begins a Push Into the 3rd Dimension. (2010, January 5). *New York Times*. Retrieved from http://www.nytimes.com/2010/01/06/business/media/06tele.html

The Fax of Life. (2003, May 23). Retrieved from Entertainment Weekly: http://ew.com/article/2003/05/23/fax-life/

The Odds of a Hollywood Movie Being Made Are the Same as a Startup Making It. (2013, August 9). Retrieved from Priceonomics: https://priceonomics.com/the-odds-of-a-hollywood-movie-being-made-are-the/

The Top 20 Reasons Startups Fail. CB Insights.

Timeline of events. (n.d.). Retrieved from Minecraft Wiki: http://minecraft.gamepedia.com/Timeline_of_events

Totten, S., & Bailey, A. (2013, December 1). *Paul Walker, Fast & Furious star, remembered at crash site by fans, friends.* Retrieved from 89.3 KPCC: http://www.scpr.org/news/2013/12/01/40683/paul-walker-star-of-fast-furious-franchise-dead-at/

Toyota corporate website. Retrieved from http://www.toyota-global.com/company/vision_philosophy/toyota_production_system/

Ulrich, L. (2016, November 7). Lars Ulrich on Metallica's Darkest Times, Napster Battle. (K. Grow, Interviewer) Rolling Stone. Retrieved from http://www.rollingstone.com/music/features/lars-ulrich-on-metallicas-darkest-times-napster-battle-w448546

Vice, J. (2004, July 2). Playing with 'Dynamite': BYU student hits the big time with his first movie. *Deseret News*. Retrieved from http://www.deseretnews.com/article/595074407/Playing-with-Dynamite-BYU-student-hits-the-big-time-with-his-first-movie.html

Virtual Products, Real Profits. (2011, September 9). Retrieved from Wall Street Journal: http://www.wsj.com/articles/SB10001424053111904823804576502442835413446

Warner, B. (2016). *Greenlight Your Book: How Writers Can Succeed In The New Era Of Publishing.* Berkeley, California: She Writes Press.

What is human-centered design? (n.d.). (IDEO) Retrieved from Design Kit: http://www.designkit.org/human-centered-design

Willens, M. (2000, June 25). Putting Films to the Test, Every Time. *New York Times*. Retrieved from http://www.nytimes.com/2000/06/25/movies/film-putting-films-to-the-test-every-time.html?pagewanted=all

Wood, J. (2014, August 28). Here There Be Ligers: An Oral History of 'Napoleon Dynamite'. *Rolling Stone*. Retrieved from http://www.rollingstone.com/movies/features/napoleon-dynamite-oral-history-20140828

Zynga shuts down OMGPOP, estimates say company lost $528,000 per day. (2013, June 4). Retrieved from Ars Technica: https://arstechnica.com/business/2013/06/zynga-shuts-down-omgpop-estimates-say-company-lost-528000-per-day/

Zynga's IPO. (2011, December 16). Retrieved from CNN.com: CNN Money, http://money.cnn.com/2011/12/16/technology/zynga_ipo/

INDEX

CPSIA information can be obtained
at www.ICGtesting.com
Printed in the USA
LVOW13*0304090418
572751LV00004B/38/P